TAKE THE
WINGS OF
A *Morning*

TAKE THE
WINGS OF
A *Morning*

Kathy Wilson

iUniverse, Inc.
Bloomington

Take the Wings of a Morning

iUniverse books may be ordered through booksellers or by contacting:

iUniverse
1663 Liberty Drive
Bloomington, IN 47403
www.iuniverse.com
1-800-Authors (1-800-288-4677)

ISBN: 978-1-4759-4919-3 (sc)
ISBN: 978-1-4759-4920-9 (ebk)

Printed in the United States of America

iUniverse rev. date: 09/19/2012

To my family

Take The Wings
Of A Morning

Part One:
The Early Years

Chapter 1

THE HOUSE WHERE
I WAS BORN

I t was May 30, 2003. I'd come back, for the first time in many years, to visit my home town of Chesterfield in Derbyshire, and the house where I'd grown up. What a shock!

The house looked bare and defenseless on its corner lot. Where was the five-foot-high privet hedge which had been planted along two sides of the garden? It had given me such a sense of security when I was younger. And where was the beautiful rose bed in front of the living-room window which Dad had tended so lovingly?

Everything was changed, almost beyond recognition, but I still had my memories . . .

**The house where I was born at Hunloke
Avenue in Chesterfield in 2003**

*   *   *

Mom and Dad lived in that two-storey semi-detached red brick council house for nearly forty years. Dad's mother lived with us for over twenty of those years, and it was there that my sister Joan and I grew up.

Even as a child, knowing that my family had lived in the same house for so many years gave me a sense of solidarity and 'unchangeableness'. This was very reassuring to me, since I grew up during World War II, a time when many children were evacuated across the country, and even across the sea to Canada.

I remember some interesting interior changes from time to time. The old fireplace in the living room had towered 'way above my head when I was growing up. It was a black metal-hooded open range, with an oven on one side, and a small hot water tank on the other. Mom dipped into this tank when making tea in the copper kettle on the hob. The open fire area backed onto a larger boiler, which provided all our hot water for baths and laundry, by way of pipes leading to a cistern in the airing cupboard in my parents' bedroom. In later years, this old-fashioned monster was replaced by a much smaller neatly tiled hearth.

It was a very exciting time for me when Dad decided to hire workers to completely redecorate the living room and hallway with new wallpaper and paint. The original rough stone floor in the kitchen and the red-tiled floor in the front hall were both replaced with linoleum tiles, which were much easier to keep clean. I can't even remember what the former pattern was, except that it seemed dark and uninteresting.

The beds in that house were interesting, too. Gran's was an old-fashioned brass bedstead with black metal trim. Mom and Dad had a double bed in their room, with a dark blue feather-stuffed eiderdown on top. That had to be taken away when Mom developed bronchial asthma. Feathers were among the things she became extremely allergic to.

Joan and I usually slept at opposite sides of our bedroom in matching twin beds. During the early years of the war, our Aunty Nell and Cousin Barbara from Kent came to stay with us for about eighteen months. The twin beds were pushed together, and the four of us slept top to toe. Coal was strictly rationed, and there wasn't much to spare for keeping the house warm at night.

Again, the night before my wedding, this same cousin and my bridesmaid both stayed at our house. The three of us slept side by side in the twin beds, and guess who slept in the middle when they were again pushed together?

Mom, like many of our neighbors, had a weekly routine of jobs around the house. Monday was always wash day. I can still picture in my mind the huge old cast-iron mangle which stood over the dolly-tub in a corner of the kitchen when I was a little girl. Mom had to get down on her knees to scrub the clothes on the ridged metal washboard in the tub. The 'whites' were boiled in a smaller galvanized tub on top of the gas stove. Then they were rinsed in the dolly-tub and put through the mangle. One day, soon after the war ended, Dad brought home a Hoover twin-tub washing machine. Gran was horrified to learn that it was no longer necessary to boil the 'whites'!

Tuesday was ironing day. I used to watch Mom and Gran putting the flat-irons on the edge of the open fire to heat. Then they would take them up, one at a time, and spit on them to test for temperature before proceeding with the work. As soon as I grew tall enough to stand at the ironing board, I learned how to press handkerchiefs and pillow-cases. It was fun then but, when I was older, ironing became the one job I disliked intensely.

On Fridays, before the new tiled hearth was installed, Mom would be down on her knees again. This time, she would be black-leading the cast-iron parts of the fireplace. It was a job which had to be done regularly, to avoid having it become dull and shabby-looking.

On Saturdays, we went shopping. Mom and Dad had known the grocer, the fish-monger, and the butcher for many years. Dad's father used to own the shop just around the corner from them. That made the weekly shopping trip into a visit with friends.

*   *   *

No, I thought, as I turned away, this was no longer 'our house', but it would always be "The house where I was born", as Thomas Hood wrote in his poem, "I remember, I remember."

Chapter 2

THINGS MY FAMILY TOLD ME

To look at me now, you wouldn't believe I was 9 lbs. 13 oz. when I was born in the local nursing home. Mom was fairly tall and slimly built, so just the process of my birth must have been difficult for her. Apparently, she was so ill afterwards that she didn't see me until I was three days old. Dad did though, which might explain why I always felt closer to him that to Mom while I was growing up.

I was born on the Saturday of Whitsuntide (Pentecost) weekend, a time of year which had great significance for our family and close friends. Mom later told me about listening, from her hospital bed, to the bands and choirs of the local Sunday Schools and churches on their annual procession through the streets of town on the Monday of that weekend. It was early June, a time I came to associate with the flowering of the wild roses in the hedgerows near our house. They have always been my favorite wild flower.

My mom was thirty-six when I was born, and my older sister Joan was seven and a half. Our parents had lost two babies through miscarriage, and there were to be no more children after me. The difference in age between Joan and me caused a lot of jealousy as I grew up, but I tried hard not to let anyone know how I felt. It seemed to me that Joan could always do more, go out more, and get away with more than I could. I later came to see that this was natural, considering our ages.

Apparently, it took Mom and Dad several days to decide upon a name for me. My original birth certificate was simply registered, "Female Child". Mom told me later that she liked Hazel, which was the name of our next-door neighbor's oldest daughter. Then one of the nurses suggested Kathleen, which both Mom and Dad liked. Most of the time, I was just 'Kath" or "Our Kath". Later, I came to prefer "Kathy", best of all. As long as people didn't call me "Kate" or "Katy", I didn't mind which form of my name they used. I seem to remember that the only time Mom used my full name was when she was mad at me for something!

One day, I asked Mom about the small scar on my right hand at the base of my thumb. She said she'd been pushing my pram along the street one day when a dog jumped up and bit me. I was rushed to the hospital, where I received a complete blood-exchange, in case the dog had been suffering from rabies. I wondered for some years after she told me this if that was why my blood type was O Rh negative. It wasn't until I was fourteen, when Mom had to have major surgery, that we discovered that Mom had that same type of blood.

The doctor immediately tested Dad, and his blood type was Rh positive. That could have explained the miscarriages, too. Nobody knew about the Rh factor affecting new babies until years after Joan and I were born.

The very earliest memory I have as a very small child is of being put out to sleep in my pram next to the rose trellis in the back yard. Dorothy Perkins ramblers climbed all over it, and I grew to love them very much.

I can also see myself sitting on Mom's lap while Dr. Duthie examined me. I was probably about eighteen months old at the time.

I was later told that he said, "You know what yon girl's got," indicating Joan. "Well, this yin's got the same thing."

It was mumps. I later found out that Joan had come down with it at Christmas, and I became sick on New Year's Eve. It must have been a disastrous Christmas season all 'round, especially because Joan's birthday is December 28.

I can also remember the last time I was bathed in the oval zinc tub in front of the living-room fireplace. The day I 'graduated' to the full-size enamel bathtub upstairs, it seemed so big I thought I could swim in it!

Chapter 3

MUSIC AND CHAPEL

From the time I was about ten years old, these two were inextricably linked in my mind.

Music was definitely in my genes. Mom's father had been an organist when he was younger, and her younger brother Bill had inherited his talent. Mom and Dad were both good singers when they were younger, and were members of the local Operatic Society for many years.

One of the stories Dad told was from that time. The choir was performing Handel's "Messiah", and had reached the "Hallelujah Chorus". Near the end, the choir sings a series of "Hallelujahs", followed by a full bar rest. This time, one of the bass singers put in an extra "Hallelujah", much to his embarrassment, and everyone else's amusement.

My own practical interest in music started in 1945. Joan had been taking piano lessons for about a year, on the advice of the Principal of the college where she was going for training as a kindergarten teacher. However, I was often picking out the tunes she was practicing, even before she could play them properly.

When Joan started at the college in September, Dad asked me if I would like to take the lessons in her place. That was the start of eleven years of my professional training as a classical pianist. Exams used to literally make me sick, but I succeeded in passing them up to and including Grade 8 of the Royal Conservatory.

I swore then that that would be the last piano exam I would ever take. It also affected me most seriously. The exam itself was not until one o'clock, but I spent most of that morning in the school sick bay, retching and feverish. The school nurse gave me sal volatile to settle my stomach, but it didn't seem to help much. I came very close to not being at the designated place for the exam at all. However, I went, and passed that exam with Honors, like most of the previous ones.

When I was thirteen, Uncle Bill showed me how to play the two-manual pipe organ in the chapel. It had a full footboard and several couplers. I felt really grand when I had mastered it sufficiently to play for an evening service. After that, I often played for Youth Services, and even some Sunday School ones.

One Christmas Eve when I was twelve, for some reason I didn't want to go to bed at the usual time. Mom and Dad were both somewhat irritable, but I didn't know why. I woke early the next morning, as was usual on Christmas Day. I opened my stocking before breakfast, but it was not until after the meal that I found the most beautiful hand-tooled leather music case under the Christmas tree. Dad had stayed up until about 2 a.m. to finish the thonging, and that was why he and Mom were so irritated when I wouldn't go to bed at the usual time.

I took music as a main subject in high school, and passed the General Certificate of Education (GCE) Advanced level exam. This did not involve playing the piano, but was a mixture of music history, harmony, and the analysis of certain set works. Then I went on to do two years of teacher training at Sheffield City Training College, with music as my major. This was followed by a year of private piano lessons (without exams!) from my college professor.

The first year I was in college, all the music students were involved in a public performance of "Trial By Jury" and "The Sorcerer" by Gilbert and Sullivan. I was asked to play the percussion instruments in the orchestra. One of the pieces opens with the striking of twelve bells, signaling midnight. That was my job, with the triangle. No matter how hard I tried, I only made all twelve loud and clear once out of three performances. I sure heard about it from my prof, too!

Incidentally, one of the three performance nights was April 1. I think it was the last one, and I came back to my hostel room absolutely exhausted. The other three girls in my room had scattered a whole lot of dried peas in my bed, but I never noticed a thing until the next morning!

The first school where I taught after graduating from college had an excellent senior music teacher, and there was a choir of about thirty students. We practiced twice a week after class, with Doug conducting, and me at the piano. The choir was so good that we entered the local Schools Music Festival. One of the pieces was "When Britain Ruled The Waves" by Gilbert and Sullivan. It ends on a top A for the sopranos, and they hit it beautifully at the Festival. We were given a standing ovation, which prompted Doug to arrange for a recording to be made. I still have that 78; I think I'll have to get it converted, if I can find someone who knows how to do it.

For a number of years after I was married, I was involved with music ministry wherever I attended church. Either I was singing with or directing the choir, or playing the organ or piano to accompany services. Music and church were both essential parts of life for me—and still are!

*   *   *

I was taken to Sunday School from the time I was two and a half. Dad and Joan and I often used to walk the four miles each way twice on a Sunday, and I always enjoyed going. We had a general session in the mornings, with children and parents worshipping together. In the afternoons, we had a short opening worship time, and then divided into classes according to age. In these Bible classes, we did a Bible study on a particular theme. Sometimes, we used a flannel-graph, or colored pictures, or made paper models to illustrate the lesson for the week.

When I was older, I went to the evening worship service as well. Our chapel was part of the local Wesleyan Methodist Circuit, so we had a different preacher each week. An ordained minister came once every three months for a Communion service. Since Dad was on the governing board of the chapel, he often invited the minister to have tea with us before the service.

Gran went with us to the evening service when she could. She and Grandad had been founder-members of the Wesley Hall congregation. It had started in the early1880's when a small group of people met in the local market square on Saturday evenings. They would sing hymns, read from the Bible, and pray together. The chapel was built in 1898, and lasted as a place of worship until 1957, when it was deconsecrated. The remaining number of members wasn't able to keep up with the expenses, and they were encouraged to move to the main Wesleyan chapel on Saltergate in the down-town area.

One of the highlights of the Sunday School year was the annual Anniversary service, for which I always had a new dress. One year I was chosen to sing a solo which had three verses. The first Sunday we practiced, I sang the first verse and then stopped.

"What's the matter, Kathy?" the teacher asked.

"I can't sing any more," I replied.

"Why not?"

"I don't know the tune for the other verses."

I blushed beet red when I realized that the tune was the same for every verse. I had sung hymns in Sunday School for several years without ever thinking about this. It was only when it came to my doing it alone that I had a problem. It took me a long time to get over my embarrassment.

My Dad was Sunday School Superintendent for many years, and responsible for organizing the occasional social evenings we had. When World War II ended, he promised us "a slap-up feast, with margarine on both sides of your bread." I had images of trying to pick up a single slice of bread with margarine on both sides! However, the meal was a real treat, especially for those families who could barely afford margarine on one side of their bread.

There was a concert-party one year, and Dad and several others dressed up as Mexican cowboys for an item where they sang "Down Mexico Way." When the curtains opened, I screamed! Mom had quite a job persuading me that it really was only Dad and some other people I knew who were on stage.

It was only some years later that I had the fun of taking part in such activities. One year, we were doing an item about different English soccer teams.

I had to run on stage, swinging a bucket and shouting, "Mucky watter! Mucky watter!"

The emcee asked, "Mucky watter? Where's that?"

"Blackpool!"

Those concert parties were fun, not only for our own chapel folk, but for the nursing home and the residents at other places where we went to perform.

Another highlight of the Sunday School year came at Whitsuntide (Pentecost). During the Spring, many of the children in chapels all across town did a course of Bible study on a given theme. Then we took an exam. When the results were announced, the Sunday School with the highest aggregate marks was awarded an elaborate shield to keep for a year.

On Whit Sunday, the children and parents from the various chapels gathered in four large groups in the biggest chapels in the area for a service of worship and thanksgiving. It was a very exciting time, and I'm proud to say that Wesley Hall won that shield several times.

On the Monday morning of that weekend, all the Sunday Schools assembled in the Market place for a worship service. Each school had a decorated flat-bed truck carrying children portraying a biblical scene. I seem to remember that there was a plaque awarded to the best one each year. A couple of older children would carry the school's banner beside the dray, while the other children, parents and friends walked behind.

The Salvation Army band led the singing, and there was always a guest speaker. Then we formed a procession and made our way around the main streets of the town center. We always went past the local hospital and the nursing home. In the early years, we ended up in the Queen's Park for a grand picnic. Then the lime trees which surrounded the circular cricket pitch grew too big for the safety of the floats and the banners, and we had to end the parade back in the market place from then on.

Yet another happy time at Wesley Hall was the Harvest Festival, usually in October. On the Sunday, the chapel was decorated with a display of fruits and vegetables, wheat sheaves and greenery, donated by the members. There was always a lump of coal, a small bowl of salt, and a glass of water on the Communion table. These were reminders that, without these three elements, life could not go on. They were also a reminder of the chapel motto, painted in large Gothic lettering above the organ, "Hitherto Hath the Lord Helped Us."

On the Monday evening, the goods were auctioned off. Anything left over was sent to the hospital or one of the seniors' homes in the area.

New Year's Eve was also special. We would have a pot-luck supper in the big room downstairs, and then play games until about 11:30. Then the mood changed. We would gather quietly in the chapel upstairs, while one of the leaders conducted a short contemplative worship service. We almost always ended up by singing,

> "This, this is the God we adore,
> Our faithful unchangeable Friend;
> Whose love is as great as His power,
> And neither knows measure nor end.

'Tis Jesus, the First and the Last,
Whose goodness shall guide us straight home;
We'll praise Him for all that is past,
And trust Him for all that's to come."

It was so good, walking home together in the early hours of New Year's Day. The stars would be shining brilliantly, and we would be singing hymns and talking about what we thought the next year would bring.

Chapter 4

GRAN

I understand that Gran met my grandfather when she joined the group of Methodists who met in the local market-place every Saturday evening in the late 1870's and early 1880's. Gran and Grandad were married in the June Quarter of 1883. After Wesley Hall was built in 1898, Gran was class-leader and President of the Sisterhood for many years.

Grandad had a shop in town which sold saddlery, chandlery, and dry goods. He worked hard, but would never call in a debt. Dad used to say that his dad had "a hole in his pocket as big as his heart." Eventually, Grandad went bankrupt. He died in 1929 at the age of seventy-three, and that's probably when Gran came to live with us.

One of my earliest memories is of seeing her sitting up in bed in the mornings, reading a chapter from her

Bible. Gran's room was my favorite place to go on rainy days. There, I could play with her collection of necklaces, pieces of jet jewelry, and cameo brooches. Sometimes, she would let me brush and braid her long silvery-grey hair. She would also tell me stories about the places she had lived, and the things she had done when she was younger. Her mother had been cook-housekeeper to a duke, and Gran had started work at the Hall as a tweeny-maid under her mother's supervision when she was thirteen.

Early one evening during the war, Gran went to the toilet, collapsed, and became wedged behind the door. Dad had to fetch a neighbor to help him turn her around. Then they carried her into her bedroom. It took quite an effort! Dad called the family doctor, who diagnosed a heart attack. She was about eighty years old at the time, and what had happened made me terrified! I lay in my own bed, weeping inconsolably. Mom came in to reassure me that Gran would be all right, but it took some time to convince me that my best friend wasn't going to die.

One time, during a concert-party at the chapel, each of the ladies of the Sisterhood dressed up in the national costume of a different country. She would tell the audience a little bit about the country she represented. Then the whole group sang a song from that nation. Gran represented Canada, and was draped in a large maple-leaf banner. When her turn came, the ladies sang "The Maple Leaf Forever".

I startled everybody in the room when I jumped up on my seat, and shouted, "That's my Gran!"

Little did I know then that I would be spending most of my later life in Canada.

Once I learned to play the piano fairly well, I would sometimes stay home on Sunday evenings to play some of Gran's favorite hymns for her. We had such good times!

She loved the old songs like "Blessed Assurance" and "Tell Me the Old, Old Story". Her real favorite was "Yes, God Is Good", but I only came to value the true meaning of the words when I was much older.

During the war, in early 1940, Gran refused to move out of her second storey bedroom into the shelter at the bottom of the garden when the sirens wailed.

She declared, "If the good Lord wants me to go, I'm ready any time. It's just too much trouble to get up and get dressed in the middle of the night."

Gran survived the heart attack and the war. A few years after war ended, she fell and broke her hip. She hobbled out of the hospital after six weeks of treatment, with the aid of two walking sticks. Then, some time after I left home, there were two weeks when Gran went completely 'out of her mind'. Our Methodist Deaconess came and stayed with her. She slept in Gran's bed and literally wrestled with her at times. For an old lady in her mid-eighties, Gran was very strong.

I was planning to marry my fiancé, Graham, on August 1, 1957. All went well with the preparations until my uncle Charlie died on July 3 that year. Gran was shocked that we would even think of going ahead with the wedding! However, we had jobs waiting for us in Northamptonshire, and a house to rent, so we couldn't change the date, even if we wanted to do so.

When Dad and mom moved from Derbyshire to Devon the year after our wedding, she followed them with the help of my cousins Mary and Will. They drove her all that way, taking two days and staying overnight in a hotel. I think that was the only time Gran ever stayed in a hotel. She didn't care very much for traveling, and hadn't been able to afford it when she was younger.

Gran finally died of stomach cancer in June of the following year. Mom told me later that she had noticed at Christmas that Gran had refused a piece of Christmas cake when it was offered. It was such an unusual thing to happen that Dad called the doctor to examine her. When the diagnosis was made, Gran refused to go into hospital. She stayed at home, with a visiting nurse calling several times a week. She passed away on June 3, 1959, at the age of nearly 97. I think I miss her more than anyone else in my family.

Chapter 5

WARTIME EXPERIENCES

Back in about 1985, my husband was teaching school in north-eastern Alberta. Remembrance Day was coming up, and he decided to have his students set up a display of the average British wartime rations.

Graham just happened to be close by when one of the boys commented, "Not bad for a day's allowance."

Then one of the girls answered, "This was food for a week, not just one day!"

* * *

So, what was it like to live through World War II in England?

I was four years old when the war started. The first major change for our family was the construction of an air-raid shelter near the far end of the back garden. A rectangular hole was dug six feet into the ground, lined with concrete, and roofed with corrugated metal. There were four bunks inside, two along each wall. These were made of chicken wire and framed with lumber. We had candles for light and a kerosene stove for heat, so we were able to play cards or dominoes, Ludo or Snakes and Ladders. The longest time we had to stay there was three days and nights, during the German raids on the nearby city of Sheffield.

Dad trained a blackberry vine over the outside of the shelter, on a thin base of soil. He also turned most of the garden over to potatoes and soft fruit. We had an allotment about half a mile from the house, where we grew more vegetables. In the autumn, Mom used to make pickles and jam, and bottle fruit. She put eggs down in water-glass in one stone crock, and sliced runner-beans in layers of salt in another. Gran, Joan and I helped as much as we could.

Food generally was in very short supply. It seemed to me at the time that everything was rationed: butter, sugar, tea, meat, coal, clothes, shoes, and even candy. Mom was constantly worried about our ration-books, which had differently-colored coupons for the various items which were in limited supply. Fortunately, our grocer was a chapel friend, and the fishmonger and the butcher were long-standing friends of Mom and Dad's. Fish was one thing which wasn't rationed, so we sometimes had fish twice a week, rather than only on Saturdays.

Our neighbors used to switch and swap coupons with us and each other. If one person didn't drink tea, for example, and someone else didn't use sugar, they would both benefit in this way.

From time to time, the elementary school I went to received boxes of goodies from Canada or Australia. The children in each class would draw numbers to decide who took home which item. I was thrilled one time to receive a box of Nestlé "Quik". Another time, it was a package of raisins. I was ten years old when I saw my first orange come out of one of these "lend-lease" boxes. But I didn't see or taste a banana until I was twelve, two years after the war was over. I had to be shown how to peel and eat it!

Britain had been getting fresh fruit and other luxury items from places like South Africa and Israel. Of course, this was all stopped while the war was on, and it didn't recover until some time afterwards.

During the war, Dad was hardly ever home. He had started teaching metalwork at the local technical college in 1938. Now, in war time, he was training munitions workers on a three week rotating schedule. The first week, he would teach from 8 a.m. to 4 p.m., go fire-watching on the roof of the college until midnight, then come home and sleep. The second week, he would teach from 4 p.m. to midnight, go fire-watching until 8 a.m., come home and sleep. I liked the third week best, as he just had to go fire-watching at night.

He sometimes had a funny story to tell us about the munitions workers in his classes. There was one about the guy who brought Dad a ruler, and asked he had one with bigger 64ths, as he couldn't read the ruler properly.

The technical college staff was also responsible for the people in the old folks' home next door to the college. If an air-raid siren blew, some of them had to go and get everyone out of bed. They helped them dress, and took them down into a nearby underground shelter. Dad had some funny stories to tell about those times, too.

There was one time when the air-raid warning had sounded, and Dad was on duty. He went to help one lady at the home who was nearly blind. She couldn't find her glasses right away. It took several minutes to locate them, but Dada eventually did.

Then she said, "Oh, I can't go without my teeths!"

That took more time. Then she needed her wallet. Dad did eventually help her into her dressing-gown and down to the shelter. She was the last one to arrive, and the warden was quite worried that she would not get there before the raid actually started.

Early in September 1939, I was promoted from the Nursery room at school to the first Primary class. Mom put my gas-mask in a cardboard box, and made a linen cover with a shoulder strap for it. I knew I must always carry it with me. In the midst of the move from one classroom to the other, I suddenly realized that my gas-mask was missing! The nursery teacher, her assistant, and several parents helped me search for quite a while. I was soon in floods of tears. I was so sure I had brought it with me that morning.

Eventually, the Primary teacher insisted, "Check at home when you go for lunch."

It was there, of course, and I never forgot it again.

Chapter 6

FAMILY MATTERS

As I look back, I spent much more time with Mom's family than with Dad's. Maybe that was because there were more of them, or maybe it was because Mom's family lived more locally, and were more involved with the chapel and its activities.

'Little Grannie' and Grandad Richards lived in a small house in the middle of a terrace of small houses, not far from the chapel. The house had a tiny porch at the entrance, where Little Grannie kept her big old iron mangle perched over her dolly-tub. It took up most of the space on the porch. I never stopped to wonder how she managed on wash-day, but it can't have been easy.

The pattern of all these houses was what we called "two up and two down." That meant that there were two room on the main floor, a combined living-room and kitchen with a sitting-room behind, and two bedrooms upstairs. The toilet was outside, across a back lane and up a steep flight of steps, at the near end of Grandad's garden. This seemed very strange to me when I was a small child. I was also quite frightened when I had to use it after dark.

Little Grannie and Grandad had nine children, and Mom was the oldest of the six who survived. She was born in 1899 and Elsie, her next oldest sister, was born two years later. From the census records, I discovered that Mom was sent to stay with her grandparents in Tipton, Staffordshire, just before Elsie was born. Home births were the general rule in those days, and Little Grannie and Grandad probably didn't want a two-year-old around at that time.

Mom's youngest sister, Ida, and her family lived next door to Little Grannie, and shared the small brick-paved yard behind the two houses. Two of Mom's brothers and their families lived a mile or so away, in opposite directions. Of my fourteen cousins, ten of them belonged to these families, and we had some lively get-togethers.

Because it was close to the chapel, we used to go to Little Grannie's house for tea sometimes on Sunday afternoons. Occasionally, some of my aunts and uncles and cousins would join us. I can remember one occasion when my cousin Brenda and I decided we couldn't wait until the meal was ready, and Little Grannie gave each of us a 'doorstep' of bread and dripping.

Mom objected, but Little Grannie said, "I'd never let a child go hungry if I could feed her."

Even though she and Grandad had little for themselves, they were always willing to share what they had.

There were some wonderful family gatherings at Christmas, until the family grew too big to have just one party in someone's house. There was always carol-singing, whether there was a keyboard or not. We played lots of games, such as: "Blind Man's Bluff" and "Sardines" and "I Spy". There were pencil and paper games, too, like "Hangman" and "Consequences".

One year, my Uncle Herbert came to our house at Christmas time, while he was on leave from the Royal Navy. This was during the war, when Aunty Nell and cousin Barbara were living with us to get away from the "doodlebugs" (V1 flying bombs) in Kent. Mom gave him a glass of home-made rhubarb wine, and he really appreciated it.

Mom told him, "You'd better appreciate it! That's the last bottle, and I shan't be making any more!"

Uncle Joe and Aunty Cissie lived in a small house a short way up the hill from the chapel. The main railroad line to London ran right under their house, which I thought was very peculiar! When we visited them, I used to notice every train rumbling through. They had become so accustomed to them that they never took any heed.

We did spend one holiday in Kent with Uncle Herbert and Aunty Nell in August 1939. We visited London for a few days, staying in a friend's apartment in Clapham Common. We were walking down Regent Street when Dad noticed the names 'Woodham and Pitt' on the door of a millinery shop. He said that the 'Woodham' person must have been from his Dad's family, as he thought there was only one family of that name in all of Britain, but I have since found out differently.

Another day, after doing some sight-seeing, we were all returning to the apartment on the Underground when we accidentally became separated in the crowd. Mom and Dad, Joan and I boarded one train, and Auntie Nell and Uncle Herbert were left behind. There were three stations on that line with 'Clapham' in the name, and we hadn't a clue which one was our destination. Somehow, we all ended up at the right one.

*   *   *

Dad's family was quite different. He only had one brother and one sister, and he was the youngest by several years. Gran had suffered a prolapsed uterus at some time after Auntie Annie was born. She's had to spend several months lying on her stomach in the nursing home, and didn't think she could have any more children. I guess Dad's arrival was a bit of a surprise.

Uncle Charlie was in the army during the First World War. There was a picture of him in our sitting-room, riding on a camel somewhere in Egypt near the pyramids. When he was younger, Charlie worked at the post-office in Chesterfield. Another young man, John Parry, had come from Bangor in North Wales, to work there, and Charlie invited him to stay with the family until he found a place of his own.

John later married Dad's Aunt Mabel, and they lived quite near our house for some years. I have a mind-picture of John, standing at his garden gate and handing out sweets to the children coming and going to and from William Rhodes school.

Uncle Charlie married a lady by the name of Edith (Edie) Henson from Henley-on-Thames, and they had one daughter, Mary Kathleen. Edie later died; Charlie remarried and came to live not far from us. Gran and I walked over to their house one day so that I could meet my new Auntie Flo. She seemed very 'posh' and somewhat 'stuck-up' to me, and certainly not very interested in small children. I wasn't really sorry when Uncle Charlie and Auntie Flo later moved to Huntingdon.

I don't know why, but so far as I do know, Uncle Charlie never took any responsibility for Gran, although he may have paid something towards her keep. I only remember going to visit him in Huntingdon once, and him coming to see us at Christmas-time once.

Uncle Charlie had always smoked a Briar pipe, without inhaling, but he died of lung cancer on July 3, 1956, just three weeks before my wedding. Gran was horrified that we didn't postpone the celebration, but we were on a very tight schedule.

Uncle Charlie's daughter, Mary, married Will Hardwick in 1939. I was somewhat envious, as Will worked in a car dealership, and drove his own car.

He gave me a ride in it one day when they came to visit, and asked me afterwards, "Did you like it?"

I could only say, "I loved it! I just wish Dad could have a car, and then I could ride in it every day."

Mary and Will kept the post-office at Calow, a few miles outside Chesterfield, and Joan and I visited them once. Will's aunt lived with them, and was very fussy about setting the table just right, and about us sitting down for tea at exactly the right time.

Mary and Will only had one child, a son they named Michael. He was sent to a private secondary school rather than either of the ones Joan and I had attended. When he left school, Michael helped his dad with the garage they had built onto the post-office, and took over its management after Will died.

*   *   *

My sister Joan married a man named Reg Holmes in 1951, and went to live on the other side of town from us. When Joan became pregnant, I would go over after school, when Reg was working nights, and sleep in the spare bedroom. I don't know how much help I would have been to Joan if anything happened while I was there. I suppose I could at least have run to the nearest public telephone box and called for help. Thankfully, I never needed to do so.

Dad and Mom moved to Plymouth in Devon in 1958, to try and recover some of Mom's failing health. She had been very ill in February, literally struggling for each breath. Our family doctor told Mom and Dad that, if they stayed in the smoggy north Midlands, Mom might last six months to two years at the most. If, however, they could face pulling up stakes after sixty-five years in the same town and moving to the south west of the country, then she might live five to ten years. They made the move, and Mom lived almost twenty-seven years in their new house.

Joan and her family followed the next year, and bought a house just a block up the road from Mom and Dad. This helped a lot when Mom became seriously ill and had to go into a nursing home in 1984. Joan was able to make sure that Dad had two good meals a day. This saved her from worrying whether he had turned the cook-stove off, as he was getting very forgetful by that time. Either she or Reg would walk down to his house again at bedtime, and make sure he had locked up properly.

Joan and Reg had four children: two girls and two boys. Sue and Julie both became teachers. Neil found work with the post office, but it was Steve who surprised us all.

When Steve was about thirteen, we sent Reg some money at Christmas to buy Joan a Mixmaster with all the accessories as our gift for her. She wrote to us in March to say that Steve was getting more use out of the Mixmaster than she was!

When he left school a couple of years later, he started an apprenticeship in the kitchen of one of the city hotels. The management paid for him to take chef's training at the Plymouth Polytechnic College, and he graduated in the top ten of his class. The hotel presented him with a canteen of chef's knives in recognition of his achievement. We learned that every chef has his own knives, and woe betide anyone who borrows one!

Steve worked in several hotels after graduation. These included one in Switzerland, one at Heathrow Airport in London, and one in Cambridge. Then he gained a position as sous-chef at a golf resort hotel just outside Plymouth. When the head chef retired, Steve took over, and stayed until his own retirement.

Joan and Reg still live in the same house, and now have nine grandchildren. The house is on a corner lot, and Reg spends a lot of time working in the garden, even though he's over eighty. Steve and Neil and their families live within easy driving distance, so they visit often. The others come when they can, and Joan and Reg are still able to travel occasionally to see the rest of the family.

They celebrated their Diamond Wedding anniversary in March 2011, with many family and friends.

**Sister Joan and Reg on their
Diamond Wedding day, March 2011**

Chapter 7

SCHOOLDAYS! SCHOOLDAYS!

William Rhodes School was less than ten minutes walk from our house, and on the same street. It was a single-storey building of red brick, arranged in a large rectangle enclosing two matching quadrangles. There were grass lawns around the whole building, and a playing field for the boys' Secondary section off to one side. In the early 1950's a technical and vocational wing was built at the lower end of the playing field. Dad was one of the teachers who moved from the technical college in town to teach metalwork there.

One quad served the Primary and Junior classes, and the other was for the boys-only Secondary school. (Some years later, this became co-educational.) Each section had its own headmaster or head mistress. When I was there, Miss Mears was headmistress of the Primary grades; Mr.

Kerry was head master of the Junior school; and Mr. Stevens was headmaster of the boys' Secondary School. I loved Miss Mears because I thought she was beautiful. But I came to know Mr. Kerry better, even though I spent the same amount of time in each division.

Mr. Kerry was the one who arranged for Mom to have extra ration coupons for my shoes during the war. My feet were big for my age, and the Government had provided for this. He also arranged for me to go to the local clinic for exercise sessions when he noticed that I had very flat feet.

Joan and I never attended William Rhodes school together, as she moved on to Tapton House Secondary School the year I started at William Rhodes. However, our cousin Barbara came about half way between us in age. While she was living with us, she and I sometimes walked to school together. I enjoyed that, and really missed her company when she and Aunty Nell returned to Kent.

There were two girls who lived on the same street who were quite good friends of mine. Dorothy lived next door, and Margaret a few houses away. However, I suffered a string of illnesses during my early school years, and didn't find it easy to make friends.

I actually started school after the Easter holiday in 1940, just before I turned five. I had one term in the Nursery room, which was a very happy place for me. We spent part of the morning moving from one activity to another: playing shop, doing housework; building with wooden bricks, and so on. Another period was spent in learning nursery rhymes and songs.

The nursery school 'day' was shorter than the regular school time, so I didn't go home at lunch-time. The staff provided a light snack, together with a one-third pint of milk, and a glass of orange juice. Then we lay down on cots for a nap, followed by story time. We went home about two o'clock.

When I moved up to Primary I, my teacher was Mrs. Peake. She was an older lady, and known as 'a bit of a tartar'. From my first days in her class, I loved everything to do with language. I also discovered a quirky gift for doing mental arithmetic. Once or twice a week, Mrs. Peake would line us up around the room just before lunch-time. Then she would fire mental arithmetic questions at us. As soon as we answered one correctly, we could go for lunch. I was quite often the first one out the door, but my skill in this didn't last. When I was in high school, arithmetic was the worst of my mathematical subjects. I was much better at algebra and trigonometry, and hopeless at geometry. I can't explain why.

In my last year in primary school, I was very proud to be chosen as an attendant in the school's May Queen procession, to which parents and friends were invited. Twelve of us girls wore pink tutus, and had wreaths of artificial roses in our hair. There were also two boys dressed in 18th century heralds' costumes, complete with wigs, and carrying small trumpets. We processed into the school hall to the strains of Edward Elgar's "Pomp and Circumstance March #2", and wove our ribbons around the maypole to the tune of Percy Grainger's "Country Gardens".

The system for deciding a student's secondary school education in Britain at that time depended upon the results of what was called "the 11+ exam." This included tests in English, arithmetic, and general knowledge. In Chesterfield, the top 5% went on to academic grammar schools; the next 10% to 15% went to technical/vocational schools; and the rest went to general Secondary schools.

Most students took the exam in their tenth year, but some were allowed to try it early. In such cases, if they failed, they could try again the next year. I was given the chance to take the exam in May 1945, just before I turned ten, and I passed in the top five percent. There were many times in the next five years when I wished I had been allowed to wait another year before doing so. I went to St. Helena Girls' Grammar school, where I was competing with girls who were up to fifteen months older than me, and who were much more socially and emotionally mature than I was.

It was tough! I just didn't fit in at all. I was flat-footed, which made me clumsy, and I couldn't do any of the sports as well as they could. Then the other girls laughed at me for my awkwardness. Since I was quite shy, I didn't understand many of the things they talked about. I just wouldn't ask for explanations, either, in case they laughed at me even more.

At the grammar school, in addition to English, arithmetic, geography, history, and general science, all the girls studied French in the first year. If the year-end results were good, we had a choice of adding either Latin or German in the second year. I made the wrong choice, and had a big struggle to understand almost anything of Latin for the next three years. One night, I became so frustrated with my Latin homework that I threw my book across the room!

In the second year, we also had a choice between chemistry and biology in place of general science. I knew I would never be able to face doing dissection, so I took chemistry. Domestic science and needlework were added in Year 3. We did half a year of cookery, with lessons in household management and hygiene, and half a year of embroidery and simple tailoring.

In needlework, part of the time was spent making a school uniform dress in green and white gingham. I didn't do too well, but the dress was wearable. The other part was pure joy. I learned to do Jacobean-style embroidery, and made Mom an elaborate cushion cover.

I somehow went on to Year 5, doing well in English, music, Scripture, and French, but poorly in mathematics and political history. This was the year when I should have taken the matriculation exam, but the after-effects of the 1944 Education Act intruded. The government allowed those students with birthdays before the end of May to take the existing matriculation exam. Since my birthday was in early June, I had to wait—again! So much for taking the 11+ exam a year early!

When I did take the new General Certificate of Education (G.C.E.) exam the following year, I passed English music, Scripture and French. I had a Distinction in French, but failed chemistry. National regulations demanded either a science or math, so I had to do another year of chemistry.

I had enjoyed my first three years of chemistry with Mrs. Jackson, especially the practical experiments. However, in order to pass the exam the second time around, my teacher in that final year with Miss Mathews. I didn't like her very much. She was an older spinster lady, and very demanding with high standards. Because Miss Mathews and I had a personality clash as well, I didn't expect any better results this time. To my surprise, I passed.

After eight years of grammar school, I graduated with passes in English, music, and Scripture at the Advanced level G.C.E., and chemistry and social/economic history at the Ordinary level. There I was at age eighteen, school days over, a respectable exam record in hand, but without a clue as to where I would go next.

Chapter 8

A Time Between

I knew that I wanted to train for some kind of work involving children, but I didn't know where to start. Then Dad discovered that there was a Methodist Training College at Westhill, just outside Birmingham. They offered a Bachelor of Arts degree program in social welfare, which was sponsored by the University of London. I went for an interview and was accepted.

Mom and I started putting together the bed linens, towels, and clothes I was going to take, carefully sewing name-tapes onto each item. Then, only ten days before I was due to leave home, the Westhill Registrar telephoned us. She had just discovered that the University of London had raised the minimum age limit to twenty-three!

This could have been disastrous for me, and very nearly was. A few days later, we saw an advertisement in the county newspaper, requesting applications for the position of house-mother's assistant in a children's home in Duffield, near Derby. I applied, went for an interview in Derby, and was accepted.

There were twenty-eight children in the home, ranging in age from eighteen months to seventeen years of age. The staff was headed by a married couple who were called 'Governor' and 'Matron'. There were two fully-qualified house-mothers and one assistant besides myself. Several other women came in during the week to take care of the laundry and heavy cleaning.

Among the children taken to the home were a brother and sister of eighteen months and four years old, respectively. They had arrived just a few days before I did. He was tiny, with beautiful blue eyes and blond hair. She was just the opposite: black black hair cut square at the back and a fringe coming just above her dark eyes. She had been tied to a chair in the daytime, and to her bed at night. He had been kept in a cupboard most of his life, and had not seen daylight for several months before the welfare people found him.

At the home my job was to get the children up in the mornings, dress those who couldn't dress themselves, serve meals, and make the beds. Each of us on staff took turns shepherding the school-age children to and from the local school, and supervising those who had homework to do in the evenings. Before bed-time, we also helped the younger children with their baths and hair-washing.

One evening, I was on bath duty with the eight to twelve-year-olds. One of the older boys didn't want to let me into the bathroom while he was bathing. He threatened me with what he would show me if I went in. I immediately fetched one of the senior house-mothers. She told him that

I was now on staff, and was to be obeyed in the same way that he treated the rest of the staff. I never had any more trouble after that.

But, within two weeks of starting the job, I was a nervous wreck. When I went home on the second weekend, I begged Dad to take me out of the place. I don't know how he managed it, but he came to the Home, had a good look around, and talked for a long time with the Matron and the Governor. It became quite clear to him that what the Home needed was two fully-qualified people, not just one totally untrained assistant.

I wasn't allowed to contact him while he was there. I was told to go and clean one of the upstairs bathrooms, a job the cleaning ladies usually did. It made me wonder about the change in routine. I only found out that Dad had been there when one of the house-mothers told me at supper time. I was able to go home to stay at the end of that week, and spent most of the next fortnight doing little but eating and sleeping.

In early October, Dad suggested I go and see my former sixth-form mistress, Miss Wenninger. She was a wonderful, motherly German lady, whom we lovingly called "Gert"—but not to her face! She had great compassion for her students and ex-students. I arranged for an interview with her, and she was totally shocked when she heard the details of my time at Duffield.

When she recovered her composure, she asked me one question: "Did you ever think about teaching?"

It set me back. We both knew that Dad and Joan were teachers, but I had never seriously considered teaching as a career for myself. Gert gave me a lot of information, and I sent out letters to a number of training colleges. The first three went to colleges whose programs started in January, as

I thought I was too late to go to one where the program had already started in September. Each of these three wrote back that they had a full complement of students for 1954-55. Then I wrote to three others.

One of these was Sheffield City Training College, only twelve miles from home. At that time, SCTC was affiliated with Sheffield Polytechnic, and offered a two-year training course for would-be teachers. Those who completed the program successfully received a permanent British Teaching Certificate.

I went for an interview with the Principal, 'Doc' Wing, and the Vice-Principal, Miss Jane Moulton, in mid-October, and was accepted. During the interview I learned that the students were housed in a number of hostels within easy walking distance of the college. Two of the men's hostels were located on Broomgrove Road, which ran alongside the college grounds. I was assigned to a women's hostel called Fairfield House, about five minutes' walk from the college, and there was a fourth hostel just up the hill from the college.

'Doc' Wing told me that the college programs ran from September to July each year, the same as the schools. Classes were given in curriculum, child education, history of education, educational psychology, and academic subjects. Each student chose one major subject which took up about half the time, and one minor subject for about a third of the time. They were easy choices for me.! My major would be music, and my minor would be Religious Knowledge or Scripture.

I was also told that, during the two-year course, there would be three periods of three weeks each, spent in 'teaching practice' in various schools in the city and surrounding areas. Each student had to decide whether to concentrate on teaching at the Primary, Junior, or Secondary level. One practicum would be done with students in a different age-range from the area of concentration.

I started my training on November 3 and, within a week, I was thrust into my first teaching practice. I'd had some discussion with my staff counselor, and told her I would prefer to work with secondary students. Partly as a result of my late start, she recommended that I do my junior practice first.

It was an eye-opener, but very enjoyable. The children were so eager and willing to learn. However, I soon found that I was not a good disciplinarian, especially in music classes. I found that having to teach new songs, play the piano, and control the class all at the same time was a real problem. In one of my later teaching practices, I was fortunate that another staff member sat in on the music classes to take care of discipline. In the third one, that was reversed: the regular music teacher did the teaching and I accompanied the class on the piano.

There were some disadvantages to being so close to home. There were also some personal advantages, as Mom was not at all well. The location meant that I could come home every second weekend. Although only twelve miles as the crow flies, the bus took almost an hour to wind its way through mainly residential areas. It was an entirely new life for me, and one I looked forward to with somewhat nervous anticipation and excitement.

PART TWO:
WILSONS WEST

Chapter 1

FIRST MEETINGS

Graham and I first met while we were training in Sheffield. The men's hostel at #9, Broomgrove Road invited the girls of my Fairfield hostel to a pre-Christmas party in mid-December. Actually, Graham and I didn't see much of each other that night, as I was playing the piano for some of the games, while he was looking after arrangements in the background.

Two Sundays after Christmas, I returned from a weekend at home to find that several students, both men and women, had been having a friendly snowball fight. Then the girls had invited the men over to "Fairfield" for hot cocoa and cookies. When I arrived, there were about twenty people crowded into the hostel living-room. I fetched myself some refreshments, as the hour-long bus ride had left me with very cold fingers and toes.

A few minutes later, I heard Graham say something to one of the girls about living in Manchester for two years, while doing his mandatory two years of army service.

When I had a chance, I asked him, "Whereabouts in Manchester did you stay while you were in the army?"

"I had digs on Plymouth Road," he replied.

"That's close to where my dad stayed during the First World War. He was classed C3, because he had hammer toes. So he was working at Crossley's motor factory."

Before Graham left that evening, he had invited me to go to a movie with him on the following Friday evening—our first official date!

We went to see "Three Ring Circus", starring Dean Martin and Jerry Lewis, and we both enjoyed it very much. After that, we started going out almost every weekend that I was on campus. In February, Graham took me to his home in Normanton in Yorkshire, to attend the wedding of his cousin Brenda. It gave me a chance to meet quite a few of his family and, of course, gave them a chance to meet me.

Another time, we took a bus out of Sheffield to go hiking over the hills above Lady Bower Dam. We stopped to eat our packed lunch in a sheep-fold partway to the summit. Then we eventually came down onto the Sheffield to Manchester highway. It was the middle of May, but we'd had to struggle through about two feet of snow on the high ground. We found the inn where the coach would stop and, fortunately, we had about an hour to wait until it arrived. The landlord's wife kindly let us dry our socks and mitts in front of the open fire in one of the public rooms, but our clothes were still quite damp when we arrived back at the college.

At the half-term break in May, Graham came to stay with my family for the long weekend. He totally surprised me one morning before breakfast, by asking me to marry him and offering me a ring with three small stones in a row: a diamond set on either side of a ruby. It was so delicate and beautiful that I started to cry.

When I went to the kitchen to show Dad, he soon put a stop to my tears.

"Don't be so daft!" was his reaction.

I was devastated, but also very angry. However, by lunchtime, Dad and Mom had both accepted the situation, after we explained that we would not be getting married until the summer of the following year. Because of his army service, Graham was only in his first year of college, while I was in my second.

We also received a terrible letter from his Mom after Graham wrote home. She asked questions such as, "Do you know what you are doing?" and "What are you going to live on?" and "How will you manage?" and "What happens if you have a baby?" Even though we had explained our plans, she still must have thought we were getting married in a few weeks' time.

Graham and I went back to finish the college term, and then divided our time between the two families during the summer break. I had a teaching job lined up for September in my home town, which allowed me to continue piano lessons with my college professor one evening a week. That in turn gave Graham and me a short time together every Tuesday evening, and we also visited back and forth occasionally on weekends.

By the middle of 1956, our parents had met and discussed a possible date for our wedding. Graham's parents were going on holiday for two weeks in mid-July. My Mom and Dad had arranged to go away on August 10. Since Gran couldn't be left alone, we decided to be married on August 1, and then have a ten day honeymoon. After that, we would come home and stay with Gran while Mom and Dad were away.

It was a very wet wedding day. Dad and I arrived at Wesley Hall in the midst of a tremendous downpour. My bridesmaid was a college friend, Brenda, and Joan's daughter Susan was our flower-girl. Graham had a college friend, George, as his best man. George was also a friend of mine, as we had known each other in the Wesley Hall Youth Club.

**Graham's parents, Graham and me,
Mom and Dad**

Dad & me August 1, 1956

I was just very happy to see so many of our relatives and friends waiting to greet us. The service was conducted by our own Deaconess Joan, but the vows were said to the Senior Minister of the local Methodist Circuit. The local registrar sat behind a curtain near the organ, where he could hear us quite clearly. That satisfied both the civil and religious legal proprieties.

We had a very happy reception at the local Co-operative store's meeting hall. There were about forty guests, ranging in age from Joan's young son, Stephen, who was two, to Gran, who was ninety-four. There would have been more people, but the wedding took place on a Wednesday, when quite a few of those invited were working and not able to get time off.

After the meal and the toasts, Graham and I cut the cake. The waitresses helped with handing out the pieces, while we opened some of the gifts we had received. Then we headed for the railway station. Some of our friends came with us, and we joked about going to 'Carlizzle' on a 'dizzle' in a 'drizzle'.

As the train pulled in, our friends threw a last handful of confetti at us. That upset the station-master. He handed George a broom and made him sweep up the mess. Once Graham and I were on the train, the conductor came to check our tickets. He winked at Graham and said something about seeing we would not be disturbed.

Naively, I asked, "How did he know we are newly-weds?"

My husband laughed and said, "He just had to look at the confetti all over your hat!"

When we arrived at the bed-and-breakfast in Keswick where we were supposed to be staying, the landlady told us she had accidentally double-booked the room for the first four days. However, she had arranged with a neighbor to take us in, and that was fine with us.

We had a very enjoyable time in the Lake District. One day, we went rowing on Derwentwater. It was a very hot day, and both Graham and I wore shorts. I came back with my legs sunburned above the knee, which made for a very uncomfortable night. Another day, we went climbing in the hills, and on yet another, we explored the area around the poet William Wordsworth's cottage.

Eventually, we returned home so that Mom and Dad could have their holiday. Gran thought that, with Dad away, she would be "boss of the roost", but Graham soon corrected that impression. We were busy sorting and packing, as Graham had been offered a job in a boys' secondary school in Corby, Northamptonshire. When his interviewer found out that I was a qualified teacher, too, they offered me a similar job in the girls' secondary school. Moreover, although housing was at a premium all over Britain at that time, they said that housing would be provided for us.

Corby was what was then called a "Government New Town". The authorities had moved a whole steel factory and its workers out of the east end of Glasgow to this south Midlands town, and were busy building housing and other facilities for them. We were fascinated to watch rows of terrace houses and blocks of flats go from foundations to interior paint in just six weeks. The whole situation was quite amazing!

The day we moved, our goods were transported by van. I traveled by bus, and Graham rode his motor-bike. Just like on our wedding day, the weather was very wet. Graham rode through three thunderstorms and, when I arrived, he sent me straight out again to buy towels. Our furniture and boxes had not yet arrived, and he needed a bath. He told me how to reach the market-place, and I came back with some towels, only to find the movers heaving my piano up the narrow concrete stairway to our second-floor flat. Graham greeted them with one of my cotton aprons tied around his waist. What a beginning to our marriage!

Things did cool down somewhat after that, but it seemed as if there was always something happening.

In Corby, there were the girls' and boys' secondary schools next door to each other on one street. There was an elementary school about a block away on one side, and a Catholic school a block away on the other side. Since there were two hundred or more students in each school, morning and evening rush hours had to be seen to be believed. I certainly disliked traveling to and from school on the back of Graham's motor-bike in that big crowd, and I walked whenever the weather was fine.

I had to go to a doctor about two months after we came to Corby. He said I should not be trying to teach so soon after beginning married life. However, that could not be changed, so he put me on a course of tranquillizers for three months. They did the trick, and I didn't have to repeat the prescription.

We made trips up north on the motor-bike to visit our families during the various school holidays. We went to my parents' place at Christmas, and to Graham's family at Easter. Once we passed that holiday, other things kept us busy, as we were planning to move to Canada.

Chapter 2

THE ADVENTURE BEGINS

Both Graham and I wanted to see something of the world outside of England, and we decided that it was best to do so before any children came along. We had been married almost a year when we started looking for opportunities to teach in other countries.

Graham first applied to Southern Rhodesia, as it was then called, in answer to an advertisement in the *Times Educational Supplement*. He went for an interview in London, and was offered a job. He asked for forty-eight hours to discuss the situation with me, as there were certain conditions to be met.

First, if he accepted the offer, he would not know his exact location until he reached Capetown. This meant that he might be teaching in a fairly large town or city, or he might be in an isolated rural area. Secondly, we could not travel together. He would have to leave Southampton in July, while I could not sail until November. Lastly, the Rhodesian government did not employ married women teachers, so I would have to find some other work to do.

Having considered all these things, Graham wrote and told the Rhodesian authorities, "Thanks, but No, thanks."

The next opportunity we dealt with together. We had a chance to go to the State of Victoria in Australia as exchange teachers for either one or two years. Not realizing what the consequences would be, we mailed our application using regular (not airmail) postage. It took six weeks to arrive in Melbourne, but we were both offered jobs. However, they put regular postage on their reply, which also took six weeks to arrive. By that time, we had decided that our future lay in Canada.

The government of the Province of Saskatchewan had advertised in the *Times Educational Supplement* for several weeks ahead of time. Then they sent their Education Minister, Dr. Titus and their Senior High School Superintendent, Jack MacLeod, to interview prospective teachers in about six or eight different locations around Britain. They needed two hundred, and had already block-booked that many berths with a Canadian Pacific ship traveling from Liverpool to Montreal in early August.

The day we went to London for our interview was one of the longest I have ever spent. We set off on the motor bike about five o'clock on a Friday morning, and eventually arrived at the Epping station of the London Underground system. We separated there, as Graham didn't want me riding pillion on the bike across the city during the morning rush-hour. I had a fairly straightforward journey from Epping to the Hyde Park station, with only one change to make. Then I walked across the park to the building in Park Lane where we were to meet the Saskatchewan representatives. Because Graham had to battle the rush-hour, he didn't arrive until nearly two hours after I did. I was so frantic by then that I almost wept with relief.

Inside, we were given forms to fill out and assigned a number. Then we were directed to a room nearly full of hopeful people like ourselves. There were other young couples, some with children, and quite a lot of single people. The expressions on their faces ranged from obvious hopefulness to a "don't care if this works out or not" attitude. The weather was hot for May, and some of the children became restless. I didn't envy the young parents trying to control them while they waited their turn for interview at one of the two desks at the far end of the room.

Some time later, our number was called, and we went forward to meet Jack MacLeod. He went carefully over our forms, first Graham's and then mine. He asked for more information about our training and experience, and also why we wanted to go to Canada. We told him about the previous applications to Rhodesia and Australia, and what had resulted from them. We explained about seeing something of the world before we were tied down with children.

After some consideration, Jack checked through his papers and offered us two jobs in single-room schools "only forty miles apart". To us, at that time, it didn't sound like a problem. It was only later, after we arrived in Saskatchewan, that we realized what forty miles of muskeg and forest with poor roads would have meant. We signed up, reassured by Jack's promise that, if a double position should open up, we would have first refusal.

When we left the offices in Park Lane, it was almost three o'clock. We'd eaten breakfast before leaving home that morning, but had to skip lunch or lose our place in line. We went back to Epping station separately, as we had come, but I didn't have long to wait for Graham to arrive. He insisted that we should travel as far from the city center as we could before the afternoon travel rush caught up with us.

By the time we reached Welwyn Garden City, I was feeling faint from hunger.

"Graham!" I shouted in his ear, "If we don't stop soon, I shall fall off the bike. I'm getting dizzy because I haven't eaten since this morning."

Grumbling at the delay, he pulled off the motorway at the next interchange. We found a store where we could buy snacks and pop, and ate in a hurry. The traffic was rapidly building up on the main road when we rejoined it, but we arrived home before dark without any accidents.

One evening during the half-term holiday in late May, we were sitting in my former home in Chesterfield watching television. The BBC was showing a program featuring a preview tour of a brand-new Canadian Pacific liner, *Empress of England*, which was just about to embark on her maiden voyage.

Graham turned to me and said, "Wouldn't it be great if we were to travel on her?"

Three weeks later, we received our tickets, and they were for berths on the new liner.

Shortly after that, we were offered a double teaching position in a three-room school at Frenchman Butte, Saskatchewan. We had no idea exactly where that was, but we found that it was located on the North Saskatchewan River near the Alberta border, in "the only province with two straight sides" on the map of Canada.

We finished out the school year in Corby in July, and then went to visit both sets of parents. It was a very tearful "good-bye" for me, as I thought it might be the last time I should see Mom and Dad. However, we promised all of them that, if we were unhappy within the first three years, we would return home.

Graham and I had booked our last night in England in a four-star hotel in Liverpool, as it was our first wedding anniversary. We both appreciated the fact that his parents were able to come and see us off. That made it a double celebration for the four of us.

Chapter 3

EARLY CANADIAN
EXPERIENCES

We left Liverpool on August 2, and had a very smooth voyage. For us, the meals were somewhat overwhelming in their variety and abundance, as we had just left a country still suffering from the results of strict rationing. Every meal on board ship had four courses, with several choices for each course. Our small stomachs had a bit of a problem coping with such bounty.

We were seated at a table for ten people. One couple was from Newcastle in the north-east of England, and another was from Norway. They soon found they could understand each other's conversation with very little translation. It was fascinating to listen to them. Two other people, Chris and Vicky, were from Canada, returning home after two years of exchange teaching in England. They were very helpful to us in many ways.

On the fourth morning after leaving Liverpool, I went topside about 6 a.m. to get my first glimpse of land on the other side of "the big pond". There was thick fog, but a huge iceberg floated by as I watched. The fog soon cleared, and we sailed into the Gulf of St. Lawrence in bright sunshine.

Graham had bought a new camera on board ship, once we were outside the twelve-mile tax boundary. It cost quite a bit less than he would have paid while still in England. He took a whole roll of photos as we sailed along the river. Unfortunately, he snapped the film as he was removing it from the camera, and lost the whole lot. We never had a chance to repeat the experience, either.

The next day we arrived in Quebec City. The liner stopped there for about seven hours, loading supplies for the return journey. When we reached Montreal, the crew would only have the passengers leaving and embarking to deal with. The break gave us a chance to stretch our legs on dry land, and do some exploring.

Chris and Vicky walked up through the cobbled streets of the Old Town with us in the 95 degree heat. At one point, we stopped at a greengrocer's store to buy some grapes, which gave me a chance to practice my French. The Canadian couple decided to do some more exploring, but Graham and I decided to catch a bus back to the dock. That was when we found out the hard way that traffic travels on the opposite side of the street in Canada!

Chris had advised Graham not to purchase a car in Montreal, as there would be a 3% sales tax added to the price. Instead, we could take the train to Toronto, in the neighboring Province of Ontario, and buy a car without paying sales tax. Unfortunately, by the time we had disembarked, been through customs, and put most of our goods in bond for shipment west, we had missed the express train to Toronto. We had to wait seven hours in a huge unfamiliar station in a heat-wave for the overnight "local". What an introduction to Canada!

Once we arrived in Toronto, we found a place to eat breakfast. Then Graham spent the next two hours on the telephone, tracking down various car dealers from ads in the *Globe and Mail* newspaper. He finally decided on the make and model he liked. It was a newly-designed Rambler American, and we found the nearest dealership. Once there, he and the salesman discussed technical details, but he gave me the choice of color scheme. From the picture-list supplied by the dealer, I chose a bright red main color, with a smart-looking white stripe across the middle. Then we settled down to wait for the car to come off the assembly-line

We didn't want to stay in the middle of the big city, but found a comfortable motel in Mimico, on the shore of Lake Ontario. Most days, we sunbathed and swam in the lake, and generally took life easy. One day, we took a steamer trip across the lake, hoping to see Niagara Falls. We were very disappointed to find that the steamer wouldn't go all the way to the Falls. We also realized that the boat's schedule wouldn't allow us to take the round trip there and back by bus in time to catch the last steamer back to Toronto. As a matter of fact, I still haven't seen Niagara Falls, except in photographs and on television.

On the fifth day of our stay in Mimico, we received a call from the dealer to say that our car was ready to roll. By the time all the paperwork was completed, it was after three o'clock. We were told to 'run the car in' at no more than forty miles an hour. That proved impossible. We had to travel on the 401 Freeway during a Friday night rush-hour, with everyone else doing at least sixty! To add to our concern, we had never experienced a clover-leaf intersection, and didn't realize that, in order to go north, we had to take a right-hand ramp and go down, around, and under the Freeway. We finally pulled off onto a side road with a garage, where a kindly mechanic explained the system to us.

We had learned, while we were in Toronto, that the Canadian government was building a new highway right across the country, but that the passage across Ontario was not yet finished. That was why we first headed north to North Bay via Orillia. We stopped along the way to pick up air mattresses and flannelette sheets, because the car had front seats which could be dropped right back to form a double bed. We also bought food so that we could picnic for breakfast and lunch, and just buy one hot meal a day.

The first time we stopped for gas, Graham automatically pulled out onto the left side of the road. We almost collided with a vehicle coming in the opposite direction. However, when we explained to the other driver that we were fresh out from England, we all had a good laugh.

Neither of us slept well that first night, and we were on the road again by 5 a.m. All at once, we noticed a wavy white line moving down the road just ahead of the car. I jumped as Graham floored the accelerator, and the skunk went right between the wheels! We were to learn later just how bad the situation might have been.

All we knew about our destination when we left Toronto was that it was somewhere on a river in the only province with two straight sides on the map. Because of the construction going on further south, we traveled via Cochrane and Kapuskasing to Nipigon. There were patches of very rough road along the way, but we were not very far from Nipigon when we camped for the second night. At one time, we had traveled with the gas indicator on 'Empty' for about sixty miles. We were very thankful that the car had a built-in 'buffer zone' which carried us through those miles of forest with no gas stations.

It rained that night and continued into the morning, and we found that one of our windshield wipers was loose. It was Sunday and, although we didn't know it, we had crossed into a different time zone. The town of Nipigon is mainly French-speaking, which just added to our problems. However, we found one small gas station open for business, and Graham asked the attendant for a spanner.

"No have," he replied.

My husband was astonished. A gas station without a spanner? Then he demonstrated what he needed.

"Oh," the man replied, "you mean a wrench," and he produced the tool right away.

That was our introduction to the differences between British and Canadian English. For us, the word "wrench" was only used for big "spanners".

Our route that day took us along the shores of Georgian Bay to the twin cities of Port Arthur and Fort William, (now called "Thunder Bay"). Then we went on through Kenora and into Manitoba. Between Winnipeg and Brandon, we traveled through our first cloudburst. The rain came down so heavily that we had to pull off the road and put our hazard lights on until the downpour eased. In spite of the weather, we stopped that night with our wheels on Sasaktchewan soil. We later learned of a quote which spoke of "Miles and miles of nothing but miles and miles". That had been our experience that day with a vengeance!

Day four saw us heading first for Regina and then Saskatoon, on our way to the town of Biggar. This was where the closest Rambler car dealer to our final destination was located. We had to stop there to give the car its 2,000 mile check-up. We reached the town in mid-afternoon, picked up some food for a picnic meal, and found a field to camp in overnight.

We were suddenly awakened about 5 a.m. by a tremendous thunderstorm. There was more vivid lightning than we had ever seen, and drenching rain. It only lasted about an hour but, when we tried to drive out of the field, we were immediately in trouble.

The ground was a muddy morass, and we had summer tires on the car. We finally struggled up onto the road, where the local maintenance crew had recently laid two feet of gravel as the first stage of rebuilding the road surface. It, too, was a miry mess, and we soon slid sideways into the ditch. The driver of a truck coming behind us stopped and helped us back onto the track, and we very gingerly drove on into Biggar and located the garage we needed.

While Graham stayed with the car, I went in search of a café where I could have breakfast. The local bakery was open, but had been struck by lightning during the storm. The baker was busy starting his whole day's work from scratch, but his wife was able to give me some toast and coffee.

Meanwhile, the mechanic had given the car a thorough inspection, and installed heavier tires on the rear wheels. We soon discovered the advantage of these. Ten miles out of town, quite literally "uphill all the way", the road was dry. Now a drop of rain had fallen there! We were to find that this was typical of the area where we had come to live.

We had lunch in North Battleford, knowing that we were only a hundred and ten miles from Frenchman Butte. We also knew from the map we had bought that the roads should be paved as far as the village of Paradise Hill, if not beyond.

Paradise Hill turned out to be a small village (by English standards) set in the midst of parkland and rolling hills. We found the local School Board member, Mr. Goetz, (pronounced "Gates"), who gave us lots of information about the school where we were to teach. After enjoying coffee and cake with him and his wife, he drove ahead of us for the last twelve graveled miles to our destination.

Chapter 4

OUR FIRST
CANADIAN HOME

I will never forget my first sight of Frenchman Butte, as we drove down the road from the east side. There were several rows of cottages along the side of a gentle hill above the North Saskatchewan River. The houses were painted in various pastel shades, with tiled roofs of red, green, or grey. The school itself was located on the top of the hill, and a square church was visible in the midst of the other buildings. We later discovered two general stores, a garage, a post-office with a telephone exchange in the back room, a railroad station and a ferry landing.

Mr. Goetz took us to the school principal's house, introduced us to David and his family, and left us with them. After a delicious supper, David took us to meet our landlord, Barry, who opened up the house where we were to live. It was furnished with a table and chairs, a bed and a dresser, and some dishes and pots and pans. There was cold water on tap in the kitchen, and an outside "biffy". A coal and wood furnace in the basement heated the house. Once we learned to use it, we found it very efficient. Barry's wife, Rose, provided some bedding, cutlery, and food, which we promised to replace as soon as we could.

We slept very little that first night, and went to one of the stores early the next morning to stock up on groceries. I had no idea how the prices in Canada compared with those I was used to paying in England. I do remember, though, that I had change from a ten-dollar bill when we'd bought what I thought we'd need for about a week's meals. Then we headed for North Battleford to see what we could buy to make our house more of a home. David had shown us the catalogs from Sears and Eaton's, and we had a tentative list of purchases.

While we were in town, we checked with the customs people to see if our bonded goods had arrived. They hadn't. Our current purchases were delivered two days later, but our other goods didn't arrive until early October. This was because we had addressed the crates to Battleford, not realizing that this was a separate municipality from North Battleford, and was on the other side of the river. Once we solved the mystery and crossed the river, we found our crates waiting for us.

Within our first few days at the Butte, David took us up to the school and showed us around. There were the expected three classrooms, outdoor toilets, a fairly large school field, and a barn. David told us that several of the students came from quite a distance, and rode horses to school whenever the weather allowed. One high school student even came from across the river. In bad weather, or if the ferry wasn't running for some reason, he boarded with a friend in the village.

I was both shocked and surprised to find that I had been appointed to teach the four Primary grades in one room, with Graham taking the four Intermediate grades in another, while David was responsible for the four high school grades in the third room. Not only had I never taught a multi-grade room, I had never taught Primary-age children. When we discussed the problem, the three of us decided to teach by subject rather than by grade. Then David had to obtain the Superintendent's permission to do this.

Once the term started, I taught reading, spelling, literature, social studies, music, health and physical education to Grades 1 to 4; English language, literature, and music to Grades 5 through 8; and French in the high school room, while Graham taught maths and sciences in all three rooms. That left David with English and social studies in Grades 9 through 12; physical education with Grades 5 to 8; and oral English with the Primary children. It worked very well.

My main problem arose from the diversity of abilities in the students, especially in Grade 1. At that time in Saskatchewan, a child starting school must be six years of age before December 31 of that year. There were seven children in Grade 1, two of whom had January birthdays. Two were not six until late in the year, and the other three had birthdays mid-year. With such an age difference, I found myself teaching them on an almost individual basis, particularly in reading. When the Superintendent came on his semi-annual visit, he criticized me for it, but it was the only way I could really help the children to learn.

There were two Grade 2 students, four Grade 3's, and three Grade 4's. Each pair of grades followed the same program for science, social studies and health, which cut down on the time I spent in preparation and grading.

Quite a few of the students, even in high school, had never been as far from home as North Battleford, just over a hundred miles away—and that was the year that Sputnik was launched! Graham and I found it difficult to believe that such insular rural communities still existed in the late 1950's. However, when planning the end-of-year celebration, David decided to take the high school students to North Battleford, and show them the old RCMP fort and museum. He knew that this part of Saskatchewan had been heavily involved in the Metis Rebellion under Louis Riel, less than a hundred years before. Artifacts from one of the battles were still being found on the hill which gave the village its name.

While Graham and I were becoming adjusted to this very different school system, we were also becoming involved in the social life of this very close-knit community. One of our nearest neighbors was a young Anglican priest, Ken Genge, who was just three weeks younger than Graham. Ken was very different from the Anglican priests we had met occasionally in England. He wore his hair in a crew-cut; he coached the local boys' hockey team; and he liked to hunt. Although he was fresh out of seminary in Saskatoon, he was responsible for three congregations, ten miles apart along the river, We thought that was rather a lot of responsibility for a newly-ordained priest, but later found that this was a common situation in the rural areas of the province.

In October, Ken introduced us to the good old prairie tradition of the 'Fowl Supper'. Each of his three congregations sponsored one of these in turn, and each was supported by the people in the whole district. This was a mixed farming area, and all the food was locally produced. What feasts they were!

Then there was the Brant Oratory competition. Each student in Grades 1 through 4 had prepared a recitation, and those in the higher grades had written an essay on a topic of their own choice. The standard of these compositions was expected to be more 'professional' in the higher grades, as was the oral presentation of what they had written. After the classroom performances by every student, the top boy and girl from each grade presented their pieces for the whole community. The best of these would go to the district 'speak-off'.

The first community speech night we attended was on October 31 in the Community Hall at The Butte. It was a great success. However, the thing that I remember about that night was leaving the Hall about ten o'clock, and finding snow falling!

There was also curling. This was a sport we had never experienced in England, but which was very popular in our new home. Every community had its curling rink, although many of them couldn't be used until the weather was cold enough to freeze the water for flooding the curling surface. It was early December that year before the one at Frenchman Butte was ready for a regular schedule of games. Ken, our friendly minister, invited Graham and me to join him on a team, together with Adolph Buchta, one of the store-keepers. Ken had curled since he was quite young, and Adolph had several years' experience.

I have a problem with balance of any sort on uneven ground, and especially on slick surfaces, but I managed to stay on my feet. Heaving a forty pound rock down the rink so as to come close to where Ken wanted it provided some interesting results. It took me almost half the season to get my rocks over the hog-line, but everyone was very encouraging—and didn't laugh too much. By the time we came close to the end of the season in March, the ice was starting to melt, and I found it nearly impossible to do anything helpful for the team. But the game was great fun, and helped us become better acquainted with our neighbors.

By late March, I knew I was pregnant, and I was just barely able to cope with my school work, never mind other activities. Graham applied for and was offered the position of Principal of the Springwater school, just twenty-three miles from Biggar, for the following school year. Such a promotion would have taken many years in England, but he accepted. We were also happy that his responsibility allowance would help make up for the loss of my income.

Chapter 5

OUR GROWING FAMILY

Over the next seven years, we were blessed with five children, three girls and two boys. They were each born in a different town, in two different provinces. This was because, for various reasons, one or both of us changed jobs and we moved house nineteen times in the first twenty-one years we were married. Usually, there was a better salary, or a bigger house, or a chance for teaching only a few subjects which we enjoyed. There were times when I was not able to find a job in the same school or even the same School District as Graham, and had to live away from home for a semester.

In mid-October 1958, I went into St. Margaret's Hospital in Biggar with what turned out to be false labor pains. The next day, our village gossip was already telling people that I'd had my baby and it was a boy. She was very surprised when the baby didn't arrive for two more weeks, and that "he" was a girl!

On October 28th, Graham had one of the semi-annual visits from the local School Superintendent. This time he was accompanied by the senior High School Superintendent, Jack MacLeod, who had interviewed us in London. Graham asked me to cook a hot lunch for everyone at the teacherage, and I prepared a roast chicken with all the trimmings. The meal went well, and the men returned to the school. I was just about to wash the dishes when all at once I felt really, really tired. I decided to leave the dishes and lie down for a while.

By 8:30 that night I was in labor, and this time there was no mistake. Graham took me to the hospital, and my family doctor came in about 10:30.

He ordered a tranquillizer for me and told the nurse, "This gal will probably go 'til morning."

Surprise, surprise! The nurse had to call the doctor in a hurry at half past one in the morning. He ordered the nurse to give me a dose of ether to keep things quiet until he could get to the hospital. (I'd had hemorrhoid surgery the previous August, and he didn't want me doing any damage while birthing my baby.) Rosemarie Elizabeth was born at twenty-two minutes past two on October 29th, weighing six pounds and two ounces.

*   *   *

The following year, Graham and I were teaching together in the two high school rooms of a six-room school at Birsay, Saskatchewan. This town is quite close to where the John Diefenbaker Dam was being built on the South Saskatchewan River. When the local school board found out in late November that I was pregnant again, they requested my resignation effective at Christmas, even though the baby wasn't due until late June.

The reason they gave was, "We don't think it suitable for someone in that condition to be teaching impressionable adolescents."

The year was 1960, and Birsay was a rural area where most of the students came from farm homes! However, I consented to stop my teaching at the school, provided I could help Graham out by taking the French classes in our own home for the rest of the school year.

Our nearest hospital was fifteen miles down the road in Lucky Lake. In late May, we rented a small house there. Graham was going to Summer School at Queen's University in Kingston, Ontario. Since I didn't drive, I needed to be close to medical facilities. We were fortunate to find a neighbor who was willing to look after Rosemarie for a few days if I was in hospital with the new baby when Graham left for Ontario.

I did go into hospital on June 26, three days before the end of the school term. By quarter to seven the next morning, I was in the delivery room, and the nurse was phoning my doctor. Before she returned, Lynne Ann had arrived. Not having had any preparation classes, I had been pushing steadily for two minutes without a break, while hanging onto the thumb of the probationer nurse who sat beside me. I think that was the hardest and longest two minutes of my life!

Graham did have to leave Lucky Lake before I came out of hospital, and the next six weeks were something of a nightmare for me.

It didn't help that he was writing comments such as, "It's nice and cool today, about sixty-five degrees under the trees by the lake."

Southern Saskatchewan was experiencing a heat-wave where, even at night, the temperature didn't drop below seventy-five degrees. Lynne had constant colic, and the doctor and I tried everything we could think of to cure it. It wasn't until Graham came home in mid-August that we were able to solve it.

He simply asked, "Did you think the formula might not suit her?"

I had put her on the same formula I'd used for Rosemarie after I stopped breast-feeding her. As soon as we switched Lynne from formula to powdered skim milk, the colic was gone and we were all able to sleep much better.

In the midst of Lynne's colic, Rosemarie caught trench-mouth and had to exist on nothing but Koolaid for six weeks. The doctor told me he could give her a penicillin mouth wash, but I would have to make sure she didn't swallow it. It would still take six weeks for her to recover. The trench-mouth had been caused by the fact that we had no screens on the windows or doors of our house, and the flies got on the food.

Rosemarie also put her hand on the electric cooking plate at one point before it was completely cold, and I had to rush her to the hospital for burn treatment. It was quite a summer!

* * *

Our third child, Donna Elaine, was born in 1962 at Westlock, Alberta. Graham and I had again been teaching together, this time in the high school at Fawcett, Alberta, twenty-three miles north of Westlock. He had enrolled at the University of Sasakatchewan in Saskatoon for September, to finish his Bachelor of Education degree. I had obtained a position in a one-room school at Seagram, near Unity, Saskatchewan. The baby was due on August 27th, but didn't arrive until September 9th. Graham had to leave for Saskatoon on 23rd of that month. In the meantime, he was substitute teaching for me in Seagram, and I stayed with friends until I went into hospital.

When I was able to leave the hospital, I traveled with another friend in his van from Fawcett to Edmonton, and then by train to Unity. Elaine slept most of the way in her carry-crib. Graham and the two older girls met us at Unity station, and we drove the fifteen miles to the school.

On the school field, a few yards from the school itself, was a tiny two-room teacherage for us to live in. The house was not insulated, and was kept warm on cold days by a small oil heater and a coal-and-wood-fired stove. Graham took the children with him to Saskatoon for part of the time, and I had them with me the rest of the time. We switched about every two weeks. In late January, the temperature where I was dropped to seventy below zero, and a blizzard blew in for a week. I was extremely glad that the children were with him and not with me at the time.

We waited six years for our first son, and ended up with two. In the school year of 1963-64, we were living at Golden Prairie in southern Saskatchewan, and the nearest hospital was twenty-five miles south at Maple Creek. Graham was Principal of the Golden Prairie school, and also teaching in the three-grade high school room. I had taken time off from school that year to look after our growing family.

On January 24, I had been very uncomfortable all day, but with no actual symptoms of the onset of labor. I remember traveling some very rough roads to the hospital for a check-up. It was a Friday afternoon, and school was out for the weekend. My doctor decided to put me in the labor ward and "see what happens" after he gave me a hefty dose of quinine. He thought that would either "bring things on" or stop them altogether. It's funny but that is the one birth I cannot actually remember, not even the time of Ernest Harry's arrival. I think it may have been about five o'clock in the morning.

*   *   *

Since I was not teaching the following year, nor intending to teach, I nursed Ernest for six months. There was only one problem: by September, I knew I was pregnant again. I had said earlier that I never wanted an odd number of children, because the one in the middle catches it from both ends. As it turned out, she sure did! Having two older sisters and two younger brothers didn't help.

Yes, as I indicated earlier, #5 was another boy. We were living in Schuler, Alberta, and Graham was the Vice-Principal of the school there. The nearest hospital was in Medicine Hat, forty-five miles away on a gravel road.

I had no way of calculating whether this baby was due on March 19, April 19 or May 19. However, I went into hospital on April 1, thinking that the baby was on the way, and ten days overdue.

My doctor examined me, agreed with my estimate, and admitted me to the obstetrical ward. He tried to bring the baby on for the next four days. I just became tired of all the castor oil and orange juice they asked me to take, but I loved the twice-daily hot baths! Finally, on April 10, the doctor ordered an X-ray. Lo and behold, I was one week short, not three weeks late!

Then there was another problem.

When the doctor came in on Monday, April 12, he said, "I was going to send you home today, but a blizzard warning has been issued. I'm going to move you to the gynecology ward for a few days. You'll have your baby for sure on April 19, if nothing happens earlier than that."

Two days later, the baby did a complete somersault, and wedged himself with his head tight up under my ribs, and his heels planted on either side of my groin. I couldn't move! I was so glad that I was in the hospital and not somewhere "out there" on a snowy icy road, trying to get to the city in a hurry.

Guy stayed in that awkward position for three more days and then, on Saturday 17th, he did another somersault. This time, he stayed put, and arrived in the outside world right on time.

Chapter 6

PEOPLE AND PLACES

From the time we lived in Frenchman Butte and first met Ken Genge, the young Anglican minister there, we seemed to almost follow each other around. Besides being very close in age, Graham and Ken shared a very dry sense of humor, and had many of the same interests. It was Ken who gave us our first taste of wild venison from a deer he had shot, hung, and cooked himself. We attended his wedding in Saskatoon in the summer of 1958. We also visited Ken and Ruth back at The Butte on a summer driving holiday a few years after that.

In 1961, Ken was in Shellbrook, Saskatchewan, and I was teaching school for one semester at Shell Lake, not far away. I spent one weekend with Ken and Ruth while I was in that area. At the church on the Sunday morning, I managed to choke on the Communion wine. I had tried to breathe and swallow at the same time, and it didn't work. I was extremely embarrassed, but there were very few people present.

Ken and Ruth moved from Shellbrook to Yellowknife in the Northwest Territories for several years, and from there to Calgary, Alberta, in the late 1960's. We came to Calgary in 1965 and, for the next few years, lived within an hour's drive of the city. Ken and Ruth came to my graduation when I received my B.Ed. degree from the University of Calgary in 1969. We stayed with them over the weekend, and the four of us had dinner together at a downtown hotel restaurant on the night of the ceremony.

Ken later became the Director of the Anglican Retreat and Education Center at Sorrento, B.C., and I went there for several Lenten retreats after we had moved to B.C. in our turn. Sorrento was the one place I wanted to go after Graham died in 1988. My son Guy drove me there, and I was able to stay in the Director's house, rather than in the main lodge.

I wasn't able to go to Ken's installation as Bishop of Edmonton on May 14, 1988, but went with our daughter Rosemarie to his first service in the cathedral the next day. The Dean of the cathedral preached the sermon, and Ken celebrated Eucharist. Both Rose and I have visited them in Edmonton several times since then.

Eventually, Ken "retired" only to spend a year in Jerusalem, Israel soon afterwards. He had been appointed Chaplain of St. George's College, and Ruth took on the matron's job. Several years after that, they moved to Langley, B.C., but I still haven't visited them there, nor have they come to this part of Vancouver Island.

* * *

Earlier, I mentioned teaching at Shell Lake. This was one of the times when Graham and I were unable to obtain jobs in the same School Unit, never mind in the same school. He had a job at Neilburg, near Lloydminster, and I was fortunate to be accepted for the Shell Lake school. Rosemarie was two and a half by then, and Lynne was seven months. I had to board with a village family for a few weeks, but then I found a house to rent. Once I was settled, Graham brought the girls to stay with me for two weeks at a time, while he kept them for the alternating two weeks.

It was in late February that I ran into trouble. The house I rented was heated by a coal and wood furnace in the basement. This furnace had a very narrow metal chimney pipe, and we'd had a blizzard that day. A clot of snow landed on top of the pipe during the night, making it impossible for the smoke to escape outside.

I woke up coughing about five o'clock in the morning, and I couldn't see across the room, even with the light on. I quickly pulled on some clothes and went to rouse my nearest neighbor. She took me in, gave me some breakfast and, later, took me to the doctor's office. He prescribed medicine for my cough and the congestion in my lungs, and told me to go outside and walk in the clear air as much as possible.

I was lucky to be alive, and so thankful that the girls were with Graham at the time. Some of the villagers couldn't understand why I wasn't in school, but walking around the village two or three times a day. However, the story of my narrow escape soon circulated, and then their attitude changed.

*   *   *

Now, I would like to say more about our time at Seagram, the year Elaine was born. It really was our worst year ever, in more ways than one. With Graham going to university, we no longer had his salary coming in. I had taken a $300 a year cut in my salary just to get the job. (The School Unit where I had worked the year before had been "black-listed", and nobody wanted to hire those of us who had moved away.) Also, because of our personal arrangements, there were some months when we had two lots of rent, food, and baby-sitting to pay for.

The school at Seagram had fourteen students from six families in seven grades. Three families were Catholic, and three were Protestant. One family was the McGonigles, whose twins were in Grade 5. Jim and Marie McGonigle looked after my girls during school hours during the weeks when they weren't with Graham in Saskatoon. Marie also brought two milk churns of fresh well water each day, one for the school and one for me. If there was any water left in the school churn at the end of the day, I could take it home. I had never in my life managed with so little water—and with an infant in diapers, as well.

When Rosemarie's birthday came around in early October, she had such a severe dose of bronchitis that I was forced to take the car into Unity to fetch some medicine for her. I didn't have my driver's licence then, but I figured my daughter's health was worth the risk. Unfortunately, the gravel roads had just been graded, leaving a ridge of loose stones along each edge. I was within three miles of home when I hit one of these ridges and overturned the car into the ditch.

A neighbor was driving just ahead of me, saw me start to swerve, and came back to help when I ditched the car. She took me to a nearby farm, where the farmer's wife gave me hot tea and a blanket to wrap up in. Then I called the McGonigle's and Jim came to get me. He also went back the next day with a friend and towed my car home. Fortunately, there was very little damage.

In early May that year, I started suffering stomach pains and had to go into hospital. Graham had just finished at university, and was able to fill in for me at the school. When the surgeon operated, he found that I had appendicitis. He also realized that I was in the early stages of my fourth pregnancy. I wasn't allowed to return to school until the third week of June, just in time to give the final exams and make up the report cards.

However, that was not the last of that eventful school year. Two days after school was out, I put some rubbish in the burning barrel outside the teacherage. Just after I lit it, a spark jumped into the grass beside it. The district had an old-fashioned telephone system where everyone had a code of long and short rings. When I picked up the phone to report the fire, two of my neighbors were "kaffee-klatching" nineteen to the dozen. I had to break into their conversation and explain what was happening. Within ten minutes, people were arriving with barrels of water on the back of their trucks, and potato sacks to beat out the flames. (No running water, remember?) It was close, but we just managed to stop the fire right on the edge of the farmer's ripe wheat field next door to the school playing field.

* * *

In 1965, a few months after Guy was born, we moved to Calgary, Alberta, so that Graham could teach at Chestermere Lake School, twelve miles east of the city. We rented a house in the north-east part of the city, and Graham car-pooled with some of his colleagues. It seemed as if, every time it was his turn to drive for a week, the weather turned really bad: blizzards and black ice in the winter; gales in the spring and fall, and the hottest days in early summer.

Our minister in Calgary was a fairly young man, about the same age as Graham and me. He and his wife had six children. Their oldest boy was a few months older than Rose, and their youngest—twins—were the same age as Guy.

Gordon used to come to our house occasionally for a cup of tea. He would walk in and ask breezily, "How goes the battle today, Kathy?"

I'd reply, "I don't know how Phyllis manages to stay so cool and calm and collected. I don't know which one to throw out of the window first!"

*   *   *

In 1968, knowing I would be going to the University of Calgary for my fourth year B.Ed. program the following year, Graham and I took jobs in the high school at Nanton, Alberta. Rose was in Grade 3 that year, and Lynne in Grade 1, but we needed a baby-sitter for the three youngest. It wasn't until a few days before school started that we found Velma Sorenson, an older lady who had raised two boys of her own. She agreed to care for our three during school hours in her own home, and she was a God-send!

She had Elaine helping with chores around the house, taught Ernest how to pee "like a little man" (i.e. standing up), and kept Guy out of mischief. When all five of them came down with chicken pox one after another, she came to our house to look after them.

You may be sure we kept in touch with Velma for many years after we moved away from that area.

There were also times, after we moved to Vancouver Island in 1972, when neither Graham nor I could find teaching positions in our area. So we had to make temporary trips back to the Prairies. One year, he was teaching in High Prairie, Alberta, and I was doing some substitute teaching there.

Once or twice a week, I would go to work as a volunteer in the local public library. Little did I know what effect this would have on my later life! Val, the head librarian, taught me how to process new acquisitions, how to handle circulation, and how to shelve returned books correctly. I loved the work, and also the chance to read whatever I wanted when the library was quiet.

It was on the basis of this experience that I later obtained two different jobs where I was teaching part-time, and acting as school librarian part-time. The second of these was in a Native school near St. Paul, Alberta. The Principal there encouraged me to study for a Diploma in School Library Science, which I did.

That Blue Quills School catered for students in Grades 7 through 12, and also offered some Post-secondary programs. As each new course was introduced, I was given a budget to purchase suitable resources. When I first arrived, the library was in a small classroom, and only had about 1800 books and magazines. By the time I left, six and a half years later, the library was housed in the former chapel, which had been extended to make more room. The collection then amounted to over 20, 000 books and other items, and they were all computer-catalogued.

By that time, I had been a full-time school librarian for four years, and this was to lead to greater things in the years which followed.

*   *   *

A funny thing happened when we made our last journey from the Errington house (See Chapter 8) to northern Alberta. We had packed our household goods into a 6' by 8' by 4' trailer which Graham had built himself. Once we had everything safely stowed, Graham hammered a sheet of plywood across the back, further secured by two planks nailed diagonally. Just after we passed the weigh-scales near Hope, we saw a police patrol car following us.

Graham pulled over and stopped.

"Is anything wrong?"

The patrolman apologized and explained, "The guy at the weigh-scales thought he saw a horse's head sticking out the back of your trailer. Now I've seen it up close, I can tell there's no way he could have done."

We parted with a good laugh on both sides.

Chapter 7

Visitors from England

We were living in Schuler, Alberta, when Graham's mom made her first visit. His dad had died in March 1964, and she came to us in September, just after the school term had started. She had traveled by sea, sharing a cabin with another elderly lady who became her good friend. Then Mom had taken the three-day rail journey from Montreal to Medicine Hat, Alberta.

She arrived about an hour earlier than we expected, and the station-master telephoned me at home. I had to go to the school to tell Graham, and he had to leave his class with work to do while he was gone. When he arrived at the station, his mother didn't recognize him at first, as he had gained a good deal of weight in the ten years we had been in Canada.

"That's what happens," he told her, "When Kath likes to cook and I like to eat.

Mom was shocked when she learned we were expecting our fifth child in March or April the next year. With Ernest still in diapers, Mom didn't mind changing wet ones, but would have nothing to do with the dirty ones.

When she had been with us for about three months, she said something about going home after Christmas.

Graham asked her, "How are you going to manage that?"

"What?" she exclaimed, "You mean I have to travel three days on the train back to Montreal?"

"No," he told her, "five days to Halifax or St. John's."

She had no alternative but to settle down and wait until Spring.

We were glad she was with us when I had to stay in hospital for nearly three weeks before Guy was born. Lynne became "Gran's little helper" at home. She would even do the job Gran disliked so much, changing the boys' diapers.

Since Mom Wilson was a typical Yorkshire woman, looking to save money whenever she could, it took a while to show her how essential it was to have an electric dryer in a house in southern Alberta. She had never dried laundry anywhere else but on an outside line, or on a rack in front of the fire at home. So, one day in January, I demonstrated.

The sun was shining out of a clear blue sky, so I said, "Come on, Gran, let's hang the diapers outside today."

She started out willingly enough.

Before long, however, she was complaining, "Ooooh, Kath, I've never been so cold in all my life!"

It was twenty degrees below zero, with a light breeze blowing, typical southern Alberta weather for that time of year. I was tempted to ask what she would do if it was minus forty degrees, but I just managed to hold my tongue.

* * *

My parents came to see us in September, 1969. Even though Mom had chronic bronchial asthma, they braved all the problems and arrived on Elaine's birthday. We were still living in southern Alberta, in Brant, near Vulcan. For our housing, we had joined together a mobile home and an eighteen-foot-long camper-trailer. The mobile had two bedrooms, and we had gutted the camper to make one large room for the children to sleep and play in.

Graham was Vice-Principal at the local school, and I did some substitute teaching as required. However, Mom and Dad were quite content to stay home with Guy most of the time, and do some traveling on weekends.

We made one major trip to Banff via Calgary, and stayed in a motel overnight. Then we went over the Athabasca Pass and came home by a different route. They were both awestruck by the sheer grandeur and beauty of the scenery, and so thankful they'd had a chance to see it. When we were driving through Golden, we were held up by a one-hundred-unit coal train crossing the highway. Dad was just amazed, as he had never seen such a sight in his life.

The three weeks of their stay passed very quickly. Dad and Guy had fun hanging out the laundry on wash-days. At other times, Dad and Mom would take Guy for a slow walk around the village when the weather was fine.

Mom's asthma gave her problems on the flight home, and she had to use an oxygen mask during part of the flight. The flight attendants were very good to her, and Mom said later that the trip had been well worth the effort. Dad never forgot it, and often looked at the album of photos and notes he'd made. He eventually sent it to me, and I still have it.

*   *   *

Graham's Mom made another trip to see us in 1973, when we were living on Vancouver Island in British Columbia. I had made a journey to England by charter plane that year, and when I arrived at her house, she had only part of a loaf of bread and some dry cheese in the pantry.

But she also had several King-size boxes of laundry detergent in the kitchen cupboard, and I said to her, "Mom, you'll never use all that laundry soap in a dozen years!"

She answered, "Well, you have to buy when the price is right, don't you?"

A few days later, I took her to London, and made sure she caught her scheduled plane to Vancouver. Graham and the children met her there, and took her to our house on the Island. Since I had booked with a charter company, I arrived at the house two days after she did.

We were living in the house we had built in 1972 on a five-acre lot, four miles west of Parksville. (See next chapter.) It was our second summer there, and that was the year we dug a well. We'd planned for Mom to sleep in the twenty-eight-foot camper trailer which I had used for one semester while teaching up-Island in Courtenay. Just to make sure it was really clean, Graham had scattered mothballs all around the day before she arrived. Unfortunately, there were too many for her comfort, and she started to choke up as soon as he opened the door. Graham and the children had to remove all the mothballs they could find, and leave all the doors and windows open for twenty-four hours before Mom could sleep there.

Like us, she found life on the Island much different from the Prairies, and I think she enjoyed it more. We were surrounded by tall evergreens, and had a view of Mount Arrowsmith from the end of our lane. We were also only four miles from the sea. Although there was still a lot of work to be done on the house and in the garden,. Mom was surprised by how much the children were able to help. Guy was eight that year, and Rose was fourteen.

Neither Graham nor I was teaching that year, as we wanted to finish the house. A well was the main essential, and we were fortunate to find a spring of sweet water only eight feet down, which filled up the thousand-gallon pit we dug around it in just a few hours.

The other major thing we did that year was to lay our sewage line straight out from the back of the house, and plant raspberry canes over it. Neither Mom Wilson nor I had ever seen such a crop of raspberries as we harvested from those vines! Twenty pounds a day was not unusual at the height of the season.

Graham's mom found, as we had, that the winters on the Island were much milder than in southern Alberta. She was quite healthy throughout the winter, but became ill with bronchitis in mid-April. She's already had two heart attacks before she came to Canada, but neither Graham nor I realized just how much they had weakened her system.

She took to her bed in late April and, from then on, I was on twenty-four-hour alert. We had moved her into Lynne's former bedroom, and a good friend of ours came over occasionally to help me give her a bed-bath. Graham thought his mom was shamming when she said she couldn't eat the meals we offered her. But I could see she was getting weaker by the day. I wasn't surprised when she soon wasn't getting out of bed at all.

It was a complete surprise when, one evening at supper time, she came into the main room and sat next to me at the table. She reached for the jug to pour herself a glass of milk, and collapsed in my arms. She was dead by the time I laid her on the floor. It was June 3, and she had been ill for only six weeks. We called the doctor immediately, and later arranged for cremation.

Graham had already been planning to go to England in early June for his first visit since we came to Canada. Now he would have to settle his mom's estate, and divide the contents with his younger brother. He would also make sure her ashes were buried in the Baptist cemetery next to the church she had attended for most of her life.

What a job it was, to clean that house! He found, among other things, lots of pattern for socks, and the yarn to knit them with. Mom had kept them since World War II, when she had knitted regularly for the soldiers. There were all sorts of sheets and bedding, saved "just in case". The house itself needed quite a lot of repairs and painting, both inside and out. Graham put the house on the market, and set off to travel. He was fortunate that the house did sell within the three months that he was in England.

He also surprised the car rental agent when he returned the car with over 3,000 miles on the odometer! She added up the mileage three times, looking worried.

"What's the matter?" Graham asked.

"Nobody travels over 3,000 miles in less than three months!"

"I just did," he replied. "I'm from Canada, and we're used to long distances over there."

*　　*　　*

Chapter 8

BUILDING PROJECTS

The idea of building our own house somewhere on Vancouver Island had first developed when we spent the Easter holiday of 1972 at Lantzville, just outside the city of Nanaimo. Both Graham and I had had enough of prairie winters and the constant wind, so we were seeking a milder climate and more pleasant surroundings.

We looked at several properties during that holiday, and eventually took an option on a lot on an estate just being developed in Nanoose Bay. The lot was located near the edge of a cliff, with a view of the sea. The possibility of building when we returned to the Island in July depended upon the road through the estate being paved by then. It wasn't, so we dropped the option and started looking again. We settled for the five acre lot in Errington, which I mentioned earlier.

We had traveled from Regina, Saskatchewan, in a twelve-foot-long Ford Econoline van, towing a tent-trailer. We moved onto the lot in the second week of July, and set up the trailer for the children to sleep in. Graham and I had a double mattress which just about filled the floor in the back of the van. We found a coal and wood stove, which we set up under the trees to one side of where we planned to build. For water, we used five-gallon casks which we filled at the laundromat in Parksville.

The area didn't need a lot of clearing—one reason why we had chosen it—because it had been cleared some years before to act as a gathering ground for the local lumber industry. So we were soon digging trenches for the footings and foundation.

Graham had drawn his own plans for the house: a rectangle with an open central area, and small rooms along each long side. We had promised the children, some time before, that one day they would each have a separate room. Now this promise was to be fulfilled.

Later, Graham would tell people, "We built that house with the Government handbook in one hand and a hammer and nails in the other."

Soon after school started in September, we had the shell completed, and were able to throw our mattresses on the floor inside the house. The first night we tried to sleep there, something started rooting in the garbage pile at the back of the house, keeping us awake for several hours. After that, we tacked a sheet of plywood over the doorway in the evenings, until a permanent door could be hung.

When we wrote home about our activities, Dad couldn't believe I would go up on the roof and hammer shingles into place. So Graham took a photo of me sitting on the roof with a hammer in my hand, and we sent it to Dad as proof.

I did a lot of other things, too, that summer which I had never thought I could—or would!

Living in a place while you finish the interior is not easy, but we survived. When the house was finished, each of the children had a small room of their own, as we had promised. It took some time to finish the plumbing and, since there were seven of us in the house, we put in a bathroom with two toilets.

The well was dug and the sewage line was laid during the second summer, and we planted a garden and built a small greenhouse. The only problem was that the deer and the birds often found the ripe crop before we did, especially the strawberries! The following year, we started an orchard with apple, crabapple, plum, cherry and pear trees. We also built two cabins for rental income.

Most of the lumber we used for the three buildings came from our own land. Soon after we moved in, we had walked through the whole lot to see what was available. There was one huge cedar tree, and one huge Douglas fir (also known as hemlock), both very close to the lot-line. Four of the children with their arms stretched wide could just circle either one of them. We had a survey done, and found that both these trees were within our boundary line. We hired professional fallers to cut them, and produced enough lumber to frame both cabins, and to provide cedar siding for all three buildings.

Any lumber we didn't use for ourselves, we sold. That brought in cash to buy other things we needed to furnish the house.

We kept that property for nine years. Graham went back to Alberta to work for part of that time, and I raised the children on my own as well as I could. I didn't learn to drive until several years after we left Errington, but the neighbors were wonderful. I was never short of a ride to town or to church when I needed it.

*   *   *

By July of 1978, Lynne graduated high school and moved to Calgary to work. Rose was working in Parksville, and staying in the Errington house with our renters. Graham had obtained a job in Bonnyville, in north-eastern Alberta, and I took the three younger children so we could be together. Conditions were favorable for new residential development, and the town was offering lots for between $10,000 and $15,000. We decided to buy one. The design we chose for this house was almost too much for our amateur efforts, but we learned a lot while working on it.

We decided to build a four-level split, and everything went well until the time came to pour concrete for the walls. The job was partway done when we realized that some of the cement being poured was running between the upright forms and leaking out through a gap at the bottom of the lowest level! I think we lost about half a load, which cost us quite a few dollars we really couldn't afford. However, it was too late to do anything about it.

When it came time to install the drywall, Graham and the two boys did the work, with Guy doing most of the sanding. Three times through such a big house made him vow he would never do that job again.

Another near tragedy happened during the Easter holiday, when we were putting vinyl siding on the outside walls. There had been quite a lot of rain the previous week, and Graham hadn't been able to do any outside work for a few days. At one point, he had to move the scaffolding so that he could tackle the next section of wall. He tested it as well as he could before actually going up the ladder.

When he thought it was safe, he started climbing. One leg of the scaffold gave way in the soft mud, and he fell to the ground. Since I didn't drive at that time, I called a neighbor to take us to the local hospital, where our family doctor took X-rays. He said afterwards that he had never seen such a bad ankle sprain where no bones were actually broken.

The house was eventually finished and sold, and we were just happy to see it go.

*   *   *

There were two other houses we built during the next few years. One was also in north-eastern Alberta, at Mallaig, near St. Paul. This was a two storey building which was set back into a hillside, about two miles from the village. Although we were both teaching at the time, Graham and I did most of the work on it.

We started in the summer when the boys were out of university and able to help us. We were able to take our time, as we had the use of a rented house in the village while we were building. We stayed in that area for several years and, for me, that was the nicest house we built. I especially liked the finish Graham put on the outside walls, with stucco covered in flat slates of variegated stone. We had collected these while on holiday, from along the roadsides of Banff and Jasper National Parks.

The big drawback to that house was that our water came from a slough a few yards away from the house. This slough collected the runoff from the peat-based forest all around us. I had to take our laundry to the village laundromat to avoid having brown stains on everything. I didn't really appreciate bathing in the brown peaty water either, even though it was really soft on the skin.

*   *   *

We had always imagined we would return to Vancouver Island when we retired. That happened earlier than we expected, because Graham was diagnosed with cancer in December 1986. It just so happened that we had started work on a house in Parksville that summer. We had the shell up, the roof on, and some of the interior work done before we returned to school in Alberta in September. This, the last house we built, was quite a big ranch-style house with three bedrooms, a big living room, and a separate dining room/ kitchen. We had a Jacuzzi-style tub in the main bathroom, and an en suite off the main bedroom. Although we had envisioned it as our retirement home, we would not enjoy it for very long.

Chapter 9

Fatal Diagnosis

It was about four thirty on a Friday morning in early December of 1986 when Graham blearily went from the bed towards the en suite bathroom and collapsed in the doorway. I have never been so scared in all my life! There he was, laid out on the floor with his eyes rolled back in his head. I did manage to bring him around after a few minutes, but he would not allow me to call 911. He insisted he would be OK. I made us both a cup of tea, but neither of us slept again that night.

Graham stayed in bed most of the weekend, but he insisted that he was well enough to go to school on the Monday. I heard later that, as soon as he walked in, one of his fellow teachers threatened to call an ambulance. Again he refused, but he did make an appointment to see our family doctor on the Tuesday. Graham was a man who had rarely been ill in his life, and was obviously trying to avoid admitting he was really sick.

The appointment was at two-thirty, and the doctor called me at school shortly after that. He told me that Graham might never teach again, but I didn't tell Graham that. Our doctor wanted Graham in the local hospital right away, but my stubborn Yorkshireman of a husband insisted on going home first and setting up his lessons for the rest of the week. He also insisted that I make supper before he would let me drive him back to St. Paul.

On the Wednesday, our doctor had Graham transferred to Royal Alexandra Hospital in Edmonton for more advanced testing than he could do in St. Paul. A message reached me at school about three o'clock, and I obtained permission from the Principal to leave for Edmonton right away. Graham was receiving blood transfusions to keep his hemoglobin level up, but the doctors were puzzled about the actual cause of his collapse.

By the end of the following week, after several specialized tests and X-rays, the doctors allowed Graham to go home, just in time for Christmas. He had told them about our latest building project in Parksville, and the specialist said it was OK to go ahead. He made one proviso: the boys were to do the work, and Graham was "only to supervise." He was also to be prepared to return to the Royal Alex early in the New Year.

On the first Monday in January, Graham received a call at school asking him to return to the hospital in Edmonton. The specialist came into the ward the next day and ordered a biopsy of one of the lumps they had found on the X-rays before Christmas. When all the reports were in, they showed three major sarcomas in different parts of Graham's body, and the biopsy was negative, that is, cancerous. Surgery was not an option.

He was released from hospital a few days later, with the option of consulting a specialist at the oncology clinic in Edmonton if he wished to do so. Towards the end of February, Graham decided to go. The oncologist checked the CT scan and other test results from the Royal Alex. He advised Graham to have a finger-prick blood test done every week to check his hemoglobin level. If it dropped below a certain point, he was to have a transfusion in hospital in St. Paul. We kept up this routine for the next three months. By late April, Graham had had forty units of blood, but his hemoglobin was still not stable.

The oncologist decided to put Graham on a course of chemical infusions by intravenous means. We went to the clinic in the last week of April for the first of these. It made him sleepy, so I drove home. Each day for the next four days, he went to the local hospital. The clinic had provided enough of the powdered chemical for four more infusions. Someone from the school usually came to drive him home. Then we waited until the last week of May, when the process was repeated. Apart from sleepiness after the treatment, and losing his hair, Graham didn't suffer any other ill-effects.

When it came time for the third series, the oncologist decided to do another CT scan first. This showed that the tumors were growing in spite of the intravenous treatment, so the chemicals were stopped. Although Graham didn't have any sign of the anemia which often accompanied his type of cancer, the specialist decided to put him on a course of the cortisone tablets with which they usually treated the anemia. The dosage would vary weekly with the results of his blood test. If his hemoglobin level was reasonably normal, he took less cortisone; if the level dropped, he took more.

Within a month, we saw a remarkable difference. In fact, Graham did not need another transfusion until October, when he came down with bronchitis. Even our final move to Vancouver Island, early in December did not debilitate him. He was quite well until mid-January, when he caught pneumonia and spent two weeks in the Nanaimo hospital.

Our younger son Guy had been studying at DeVry Computer College in Calgary for the previous eighteen months, and would graduate on February 28, 1988. We had promised to attend his graduation if his dad was well enough to make the trip. We knew that traveling from the coast to an altitude of 3,000 feet or more would have an effect on Graham's lungs. Neither the weather nor the roads at that time of year were reliable for traveling, especially through the mountains.

We took Graham's pick-up, as we were going to help Guy move from Calgary to Victoria after graduation. My car would not have been big enough for that. But the pick-up had a standard gear-shift, and I could not drive it. I had only learned how to drive vehicles with an automatic gear box.

We left the Island on Wednesday 24th, and everything went well for the first two days, with overnight stops at Merritt and Golden. It was while we were in the motel in Golden that Graham suddenly found he could not keep any food down. He was also spiking an unusually high temperature. He would not let me call 911, but he did stay in bed at the motel for another day.

Four of our family were living in Calgary at that time. I telephoned them to say that we might not arrive in time for the ceremony on Saturday. I told them we would go directly to Lynne's house as soon as we could.

The next day, Graham managed to eat a light breakfast, and then climbed into the pick-up. I still don't know how he was able to drive for four hours over the mountain roads to Calgary, with snow coming down and many of the roads quite icy. We finally arrived at Lynne's place about half past three in the afternoon, and made up a bed for Graham on the chesterfield in the living-room. The family came to see him in the evening, but they could tell he was very weak.

I went to bed about ten o'clock, but Graham called me less than four hours later. He was having trouble breathing, and needed to use the portable oxygen bottle we were carrying with us. I settled him down with the mask on, and called the ambulance, without consulting him. He grumbled at me loudly enough to waken Lynne and Dennis, but they sided with me. I found out later that he'd been afraid of getting cold while being transferred from the house. However, the ambulance crew brought warm blankets and more oxygen, and we were soon on our way to Foothills Hospital.

Once in the emergency ward, the doctor on duty made an examination, asked me about Graham's medical history, and contacted every doctor who had treated him during the previous fifteen months. He gave Graham cortisone by intravenous line, and at least two units of blood. He also ordered X-rays and an ultrasound examination, and called in a chest specialist.

When this doctor saw the test results, he took me aside and asked, "If this goes bad on us, how much do you want us to do for your husband?"

This shocked me thoroughly, as I hadn't realized the true seriousness of what was happening. I told him that, some time earlier, we had discussed what we thought was a "remote possibility". Graham had decided he didn't want to be kept alive solely by machines, but wished to die in peace and with dignity.

Soon after nine o'clock on the Monday morning, orderlies moved Graham into a semi-private ward on the sixth floor of the hospital. He seemed unusually accepting of the situation, and didn't have the energy to complain. There was a ward kitchen nearby where I could make tea, but Graham was soon asking for chipped ice rather than a hot drink.

By early evening I needed a break, as I hadn't slept much for the past three nights. I called each of the children with an update on their dad's condition. Rose and Ernest both came to the hospital and stayed with him for about an hour each, while I went back to Lynne's. I still could not sleep, but I did rest for a while, and was back in the hospital by ten o'clock.

About half an hour after I returned, Graham fell asleep for a short time.

When he woke, he said something very unusual for him: "Guess I was out on Cloud Nine there for a while."

I didn't know quite what to make of that, but I was glad he's had some kind of vision, perhaps of Heaven.

Graham died about three thirty the next morning, in peace and with dignity, just as he had wished. I had to authorize an autopsy, since he had been in the hospital less than forty-eight hours, and that was their policy. Then my daughter Lynne and I arranged for cremation. I flew home on the Tuesday afternoon.

Elaine and her family met me at the Nanaimo airport, and young John nearly broke my heart with his first question: "Where's Poppa?"

Elaine explained to him that Poppa was now with Jesus in Heaven, and would not be coming home again, ever—pretty tough for a four year old to understand and accept.

Chapter 10

PICKING UP THE PIECES

Our minister called a few days later to arrange a memorial service. It was held a week after that, at St. Anne's Anglican Church, and the family and I helped each other through. The whole family was there, including the two young men we had fostered at different times in the past.

The pastor spoke about Graham's family and his job. He elicited a smile from everyone when he mentioned a sixth "baby" which Graham had "birthed". This was the book he had written shortly before he died.

Graham and I had discussed pension arrangements during the previous summer, and I knew I would be able to live quite comfortably on the monthly payment which would be made by the Alberta Teachers' Federation for the rest of my life. I also had a good idea about "who would get what" of Graham's personal items, and the family was not disposed to quarrel with his last wishes.

Once the memorial service was over, I started making plans. First of all, I needed a few days alone. As I mentioned earlier, I had spent a couple of Lenten Retreat periods at the Anglican Retreat Centre at Sorrento, B.C., and I knew that our old friends Ken and Ruth Genge were now the Directors there. Graham had willed his pickup to Ernest, who already had a truck. So Ernest sold it to Guy for one dollar. Guy and his wife, Lila, had been living in Calgary when Graham died, but were now settled in Victoria, B.C. Now Guy offered to take me to Sorrento on his way back to Calgary to fetch the last of their things.

Before he left me at Sorrento, Guy said, "Take your time, Mom. Give me a call when you're ready to go home." I stayed five days, sleeping in the basement suite in the Director's house, rather than in the main Lodge where people on retreat were accommodated. I played Ruth's piano from time to time, wandered down by the lake, and rested as much as I thought I needed to do. I was also able to eat three goods meals a day which I didn't have to prepare or clean up, and felt much better by the time Guy came to take me home.

In April, I took another couple of days at a local hotel with a view of the Strait of Georgia. I was looking out the window of the dining room one evening, when I felt encouraged to write a poem. I called it simply "A Tribute":

Grey; all is grey:
Grey sky;
Great grey sea;
Grey hills
Moving in and out of grey mist
Across the bay.

But, all at once,
A flight of birds
skims the swelling sea.
They, too, are grey,
Scarcely darker than the sea itself.

Then the clouds part.
A single shining ray
Lights up the restless sea—
A reminder of a light once seen
When I was partway there,
Only to return again. *
And shining rays of light—
You, too, were partway there,

That last night.
"Out on Cloud Nine,"

you said.

I knew exactly what you meant.
What a vision it was for you . . .
Much like mine many years ago,
I suspect.

Each of us
has our own vision
of Heaven

I came back
For many years more,
It seems.
You . . .
you only had a few hours
Before you slipped away,
for ever.

But you went so peacefully,
With dignity, without pain—
just the way you wished.

And life for me was grey . . .
but not **all** grey:
There are flights of birds

More and more as the days go
on.

I'm not sure if you believed
before.
But I am sure
that we shall meet again.
We shall be a part
of that glorious vision.
In fact, I don't just believe;
I know!

[*See Part 3, Chapter 1]

I decided I could not stay in the house we had built in Parksville, so I leased it to our daughter Elaine and her family. They had already been living with us for some time, helping with the finishing work on the house. Elaine had done much of the interior painting while Steve looked after the electrical wiring and fittings. I moved into a local motel for the time being.

In May, I bought a cottage at Beach Acres Resort, south of Parksville. It was only half-finished at the time, but I was able to tour one of the completed ones built on the same pattern as the one I had chosen for its location. I moved in on June 1. There was an indoor pool in the office building, where I swam several mornings a week. I also walked on the golden sand beach at low tide, and watched the deer as they wandered through the property—and I was only five minutes' drive from town.

Before he died, Graham and I had also talked about taking a cruise to Alaska in July of 1988, if he was well enough. Now I decided to do it anyway. I needed a complete change of people and places after all the recent upsets, so what better way to get it? I registered with a Christian travel group based in Toronto, and joined them in Vancouver. We started with a guided tour of the city. Although I was already familiar with the downtown area, I saw a few things that day which I hadn't seen before.

The *Viking Star* left Vancouver just before six in the evening, and we were sailing calmly past my beach-front home while eating dinner. I felt pampered and completely relaxed. I teamed up with an elderly Texas gentleman for square dancing, which was scheduled every afternoon that we were in a port. I hadn't square danced for quite a few years, but my feet hadn't forgotten the moves.

Ted said to me one time (about the dancing): "I trust you because you seem to know what you're doing."

I found out later that Ted was over eighty and had a girl-friend in Montreal! He was a retired civil engineer, apparently had lots of money, and loved to spoil me. When we stopped in Sitka, we went window-shopping together. He noticed that I was admiring an aqua-colored sweat shirt with a white seal-pup on the front.

"Go try it on," he urged me.

It fitted, and he bought it for me.

We stayed in touch for several years afterwards, but he was never able to come to Vancouver Island for a visit.

*   *   *

I had booked one of my periodic visits to Britain for later that summer, and left on August 22. Although I grew up in Derbyshire, Dad had moved to Plymouth in Devon in 1958. My sister Joan and her family followed him the next year, so I was able to visit them all at the same time. I stayed with Joan, but Dad's house was only a block away on the same street, so I spent quite a bit of time with him as well.

It was quite a trip! I took a coach tour of Scotland, which included a visit to the Isle of Skye. I had only been north of the border briefly once before, and found this longer visit very interesting. I also spent three days in York. Graham and I had been there in 1981, soon after the start of a major archaeological dig in the city centre. This time, I was able to go to Coppergate and experience the "Jorvik" project, which had been developed from that exploration.

I went back to my old home town for the first time in many years, and found it interesting to see all the modern changes. It gave me a chance to meet up with several of my cousins whom I had not seen since I left England thirty years before. I also took another coach tour, to a part of England I had never seen: Rye, Brighton, and Portsmouth, and then on to the more familiar West Country. I was back home by early October, tired but very satisfied with my time away.

Indeed, I did do a lot of traveling that first year I was on my own. It may just have been the exhilaration of having plenty of money to spend and nobody looking over my shoulder. It may have been that I was trying to avoid facing the reality of widowhood.

I left again just after Christmas for a coach tour of Washington, Oregon, and California. This included stops in Seattle, Sacramento, and Anaheim. In Sacramento, the hotel where we stayed had a huge Christmas tree in the lobby, which was covered in teddy-bears. They would be given to the local children's hospital early in the New Year. We had three days in Anaheim, including a visit to the annual Rose Bowl Parade on New Year's Day. Then we went to San Francisco and south to Ensenada on the Baja Peninsula.

Ensenada was a joy, for the most part. For the first time in my life, I saw banana palms growing naturally. There was one right beside the motel swimming pool. About five o'clock in the morning on our second day there, a cloudburst broke over the town. When I went out walking later, I found one of the main streets completely flooded at one point. There were torrents of water also pouring down a bridge-covered channel in mid-street, and rushing into the sea about a hundred yards away.

The tour coach brought us home via Sondheim, a Norwegian-style village with some fascinating carvings on the buildings. Our last stop was in Eugene, Oregon. It had been another wonderful trip!

The following few months were somewhat quieter. The poem I had written soon after Graham died was published in *The Anglican Journal.* That was my first taste of "writing fever", which was encouraged some years later when I took a writing course in Children's Literature by correspondence.

By September 1989, my whole life had turned around. I was on a completely different track, but that's a different part of my story.

PART THREE:
ODYSSEY FOR ONE

Chapter 1

THE VISION AND
WHAT FOLLOWED

I n 1967, when we were living in Nanton, Alberta, I had
to go into hospital in Calgary for what was supposed
to be minor surgery. The operation took place on a
Friday morning, and early on Saturday afternoon, I started
to hemorrhage. The surgeon had gone to a weekend
conference in eastern Canada, and my family doctor was
looking after his patients. Apparently, he didn't believe the
ward sister when she phoned and told him she couldn't stop
my bleeding.

The doctor finally came on his rounds about ten o'clock
in the evening. I was literally starting to drift in and out of
consciousness. It seemed that I was floating above my bed,

looking down on myself as the doctor and his assistants entered the ward.

I cannot really explain what happened next, but I saw a brilliant light shining towards me from a large 'doorway'. Then I realized that I was being drawn towards it.

My progress stopped when I became aware of the words in my head, "Your time is not yet."

Meanwhile, the doctor had examined me, and decided, "This girl needs stitches."

The next thing I really knew, I was back on the operating table with the anesthetist pushing a needle into my arm for the second time in forty-eight hours. I flinched.

"Didn't go in quite so easy that time, did it?" he asked as I drifted into unconsciousness.

Over the months and the years since then, I have been assured in various ways that I was brought back for a reason. It has also become clear that this purpose would be worked out in some kind of ministry. Soon after my recovery from the surgery, I realized that I probably could not take on any more church work than what I was already doing: choir leadership; lay reading, and Bible study leadership.

One evening when I was talking things over with Graham, I said, "I wish I <u>could</u> do more in the way of church work."

He immediately complained, "You're doing too much already, so far as I'm concerned."

The subject was dropped for the time being, but by no means forgotten.

After he died, and I'd had time to pray and make some plans, I applied to the Vancouver School of Theology (V.S.T.) for admission to either the Master of Theological Studies (M.T.S.) program, or the Master of Divinity (M.Div.) degree. I had interviews with Bishop Shepherd in

Victoria, and with June Bradley, the Registrar at VST. I also made a flying trip to Edmonton to discuss the situation with my old friend Ken Genge, who had supplied one of my references.

On May 11, I heard that I had been accepted for the M. Div. course. I also found out that I could complete it in three years, if I felt able to do so, or I could take an extra year without penalty.

My first year at VST started in September of 1989. It was thirty-five years since I had done any serious studying, and I found it difficult to concentrate for long periods of time. However, I had lots of encouragement from June Bradley, the Anglican Chaplain John Blyth, other staff, and my fellow students. Given the choice of concentrating on Biblical Studies, Ordained Ministry, or Social Ministry, I chose the last of these. I had never felt I was to become an ordained minister, but the social aspects of church work really appealed to me.

VST is an unusual seminary because it includes Anglican, United Church, Presbyterian, and other church denominations all working together. I settled into a routine of worship, academic classes, small group meetings, and workshops. I found that mixing with students and staff of other denominational backgrounds was stimulating. There was another unusual factor: assignments were not graded by letter or percentage. Instead, they were classed as either "Ungraded" or "Passed".

In that first year, my accommodation was in a small suite in the main building, which faced out towards the sea. It had a combined living-room and kitchen, a bedroom and a small bathroom. There was a laundry in the basement, with a sign-up list for use. I could make my own meals in my room, or go to the campus cafeteria. Most of the students ate breakfast and supper together in the cafeteria, and looked after their own lunch, so I decided to do the same.

The first term ended a week before Christmas, and I was able to spend the holiday with some of my family in Calgary. My oldest daughter Rose and I went to midnight mass on Christmas Eve at the Catholic Cathedral near her home. Then we all spent Christmas Day together.

I stayed in Calgary until January 2, 1990, when I returned to VST for a concentrated three-week course in Hebrew. This was the only time when all the students had to study either Greek or Hebrew, regardless of their field of concentration. The final transition exam was easier than I expected, and I passed with quite a high mark. Then I was able to have almost a week at home before the second term started.

As a first-year student, in the second semester I began to be actively involved in community worship services and special Anglican celebrations. I loved it! I had done some lay-reading in the church at home and, as a former teacher, speaking to a congregation didn't scare me at all. Only third and fourth-year students did any preaching, but the rest of us helped with lectionary readings, distribution of Communion, and music.

I found it hard to believe how fast that first year went. I had been working as a volunteer in the Theological Library on campus two evenings a week during the term. When the staff were preparing for Summer School, they asked if I would stay on and work full-time in the Library for two months. This turned out to be a major factor in deciding the direction of my life a few years later.

It felt really weird to be on campus that summer, but not going to any classes. However, it was great to be able to meet the summer students. Many of them were active ministers and pastors, and quite a few came from overseas. There were also a number of Native trainee-ministers, who had been studying at home during term time, with the help of a special television link-up.

1990 was one of those years when the village of Oberammergau in Austria put on their world-renowned Passion Play. Almost everyone in the village takes part, but it is only performed every ten years. This time, I was determined to be there. I joined a Christian travel group out of Toronto for the seventeen-day Alpine Europe tour, which included a visit to the day-long presentation in Oberammergau. I shall never regard the taking of Communion in the same way again. Just seeing that performance gave me new impetus for my second year at VST.

The second year was much more serious than the first one had been. The most difficult part for me was a series of assignments for the New Testament course. We were asked to choose a parable, and produce an outline of how we would prepare it for a sermon. I thought I had followed the instructions given by my professor, but my paper kept coming back "Ungraded". I finally gave up in despair, and never did complete that particular requirement.

One of the highlights in the second year for me was a trip I made with the VST choir and our director, Dr. Gerald Hobbes, in late October. We car-pooled to Port Hardy at the northern tip of Vancouver Island, where we gave a program for the people of Port Alice, Port McNeil and Port Hardy in the combined Anglican/United Church.

The United Church mission boat, *Thomas Crosby IV* was supposed to pick us up the next morning, but she was storm-bound at Rivers Inlet on the mainland. Gerald arranged for a nine-seater Otter airplane to take us in three groups to join the *Thomas Crosby* at Bella Bella on the mainland coast. The *Thomas Crosby* was the latest of the United Church Mission ships serving the coastal communities and the islands off the west coast of British Columbia.

We visited eight Native communities in as many days, giving programs of hymns, readings and prayers in the villages of Bella Coola, Haisla, Klemtu, and Kitimaat, among others. Everywhere we went, we were wonderfully fed with many Native dishes after the service. At one Communion service, the elements consisted of bannock and herbal tea, rather than bread and wine or grape juice. We were also royally entertained by Native dancers, singers and musicians. It was a wonderful break from college routine, and something of an eye-opener for many of us.

By the end of that school year, I was getting rather stressed out, but I had signed up to do a three-month Chaplaincy Internship at Foothills Hospital in Calgary, starting in May. I had chosen Calgary over Edmonton for this course, so that I was able to stay with my daughter Lynne. Her house in the northwest part of the city was only about five minutes drive from the hospital.

There were twelve of us in the class, from several different denominations and walks of life. We were divided into two groups under separate supervisors, and each of us was assigned two wards to serve as chaplain interns. I was given an oncology ward, and a women's surgery ward.

In the wards, we were responsible for following patient records, studying patient charts, and talking to new patients. We had to make regular reports to our supervisors, have a one-on-one interview with them once a week, and join in group discussions on various topics connected with chaplaincy work. We also held our own weekly chapel services, and attended any baptisms and funerals which occurred within the hospital. In addition, we each spent one weekend 'on call', sleeping in a special room set aside for this purpose. I'm not sure just how I would have responded if I had been called while I was on duty, but I didn't have to find out.

It was a very busy schedule, and I really wasn't ready for it after my second difficult year at VST.

Don, my supervisor, actually said to me during one weekly interview, "I don't think you have come here to work as a chaplain. You have come to continue your grieving process."

Yes, this was the same hospital where Graham had died just over three years before, and Don believed that had played a major part in my choice of location for the course.

Whatever the reasons, by the time I returned to Vancouver Island towards the end of July, I was totally exhausted, and wondering what to do next.

Chapter 2

RECOVERY

I was involved in a car accident just before leaving Calgary after the chaplaincy course, which left me without a vehicle. That meant I had to fly home. One of the first things I did after I arrived was to find and purchase another vehicle. I was fortunate to locate one, at a price I could afford, within a few days of being back on Vancouver Island.

The most important thing for my own well-being was to get right away from home for a while, so I went to Seattle. I had never been there before, but I traveled by ferry from Victoria. I had booked a room in a hotel within walking distance of downtown, and I did most of the popular touristy things: visiting the Space Needle and the Pike Street Market. I also took an underground walking tour, as I was interested to see how the city used to look, and to hear some of the colorful stories about the early days. Best of all, I was able to sleep in for as long as I wanted in the mornings.

Once I returned home, I made an appointment to see the Bishop in Victoria and let him know what had happened during my second year at VST. and in Calgary. He listened with sympathy, and could see I was still quite badly stressed out. He agreed that it would not be in my best interest to return to VST for at least a year. He was good enough to draw on his discretionary fund so that I could spend a week at Prince of Peace Priory and Retreat Center in Chemainus.

That was just what I needed! It was a week of almost total peace and quiet. There was only one other couple using one of the cabins next to the chapel. I had a room in a guest house across the road from the Priory, and could come and go as I pleased. Father Cyril and Sister Mary Martha conducted a Eucharist service in the chapel each morning. Apart from this, and eating supper with them, I could read, meditate, listen to music, go for walks, and even sleep if I felt like it. It was a "time out of time", and I fully appreciated it.

It took me some further time after that to realize I wouldn't be going back to VST at all, and I felt somewhat at a loose end. In September, I made a quick trip back to Mallaig School to present a bursary in Graham's name to the student with the highest combined marks in mathematics and science. I intended to do this for ten years, but unfortunately I had to stop after five. That first time I went, I also gave the school librarian copies of two very different books which Graham had written during the last few years of his life.

One of these was an inquiry into the remarkable arrangements of the standing stone (megalith) sites in Britain. Graham had noticed that many of them were located three in a row across many miles of country, and for many more their locations formed equilateral or isosceles triangles. He had visited many of the sites and, in the book, provided his own illustrations and diagrams, as well as Appendices with computerized calculations of radians and degrees to prove his theory.

The other book he had written was a novella about a threatened attack on the Revelstoke Dam in central British Columbia. Again, he had visited the site, and drawn his own illustration of the dam.

Although the books were soft-covered and spiral-bound, the librarian was happy to have them as mementoes of a colleague who had spent nine years teaching in Mallaig.

I had kept up my work with the local Anglican Church, and had in fact increased my participation by going to Morning Prayer several days a week. This was something I felt compelled to do, especially since I had been to Oberammergau in 1990. Seeing that enactment of the Last Supper, Crucifixion and Resurrection of Christ had convinced me that I needed to be more faithful in my service to and within the church.

Another thing which gave me a definite sense of new life was taking regular piano lessons again, after a thirty-year hiatus. Neither my teacher nor I was interested in my achieving concert-standard performance. I had simply asked her to help me improve my technique, rather than the level of the pieces I played. However, Dottie worked me hard, introducing me to such challenges as Brahms' *Two Intermezzi* and the Debussy *Arabesques*. I kept up the lessons for a year, and found that it was marvelous therapy for me.

In March 1992, I returned to Sorrento Center for a Lenten Retreat. Knowing that the weather conditions could be quite severe in that area at that time of year, I didn't drive myself but traveled by Greyhound bus from Vancouver. I arrived two days early, but was able to help the staff tidy up the grounds while I waited for the Retreat to begin.

The theme of the Retreat was "The Body of Christ", and was led by the then Director of Sorrento. We had Morning Prayer after breakfast, then a teaching session followed by Eucharist. There was time for a rest and meditation after lunch, then another teaching session. The evening meal was served at five thirty, and there was one more teaching session in the evening. This sounds like a very busy program, but I found it remarkably relaxing and spiritually very satisfying. I was even more blessed when a fellow retreatant drove me all the way back to Vancouver to catch the ferry to the Island.

Looking back, I could see that I had grown considerably in faith during my time at VST and through the chaplaincy training, and since. I was encouraged by those with more experience of the Christian life than I had. I had encountered a variety of cultures, and learned something useful from each one. My time at Prince of Peace Priory and on retreat had given me a chance to reflect on these things, and to form a new and more realistic picture of how I could proceed in the future.

Chapter 3

THE NEXT STEP

T he next major change in my life started in July
1993. One Sunday morning, our minister at St.
Mark's was talking about various different mission
organizations, including one called 'Youth With A Mission',
or YWAM for short. This is an organization which was
started in the 1960's by a man named Loren Cunningham.
His initial aim, in response to a vision he'd had, was to train
young people and adults as missionaries to the nations of
the world where the Gospel is little known. It has since
become much more than that.

There is a basic Discipleship Training School, (DTS),
which every student goes through. Then there are different
'colleges' providing courses in the seven 'mind molders' of
education, business, the arts, religion, family, government,
and communications.

Kathy Wilson

What interested me was the fact that they also have volunteer workers, who can go to a YWAM campus for anywhere from three weeks to three months at a time. There, they work as plumbers, carpenters, mechanics, telephone receptionists, secretaries, child-care workers, cooks, cleaners, hospitality people, maintenance, gardeners and grounds-keepers. Each department has one or more staff people responsible for assigning and supervising the work.

YWAM bases and offices have now been set up in almost 200 countries around the world. In many cases, all the volunteers need is their airfare and personal expenditures. Accommodation and meals are provided. Many of these 'Mission Builders' are retired, but not all. Some are young people seeking a worthwhile job while considering their next step in life. What is truly remarkable is that nobody in YWAM, from the chancellor on down, is paid a salary. Everyone is self-supporting or mission-supported.

I heard what our minister said about YWAM that Sunday in July, but at the time I didn't feel that I had any useful skills to offer. How wrong I was!

2012 Photo of Loren Cunningham
Founder of YWAM

[For a more detailed account of Youth With A Mission, see the Appendix]

In October and November of that year, Alan and Vivian Lockhart, two of my friends at St. Mark's, went to the YWAM base in Kona, Hawaii, as Mission Builders for six weeks. After their return, in early December, Vivian came to our ladies' breakfast Bible study group to tell us about her experiences.

Before the meeting broke up, she turned to me and said, "You know, Kathy, they're just praying for someone with library skills to go to Kona."

I was flabbergasted, and all I could say was, "I'll pray into it."

I did, but I compromised by praying, "I'm willing to go if you want me to, Lord, but I need confirmation."

The following Sunday, all the lessons at the church were about being called to follow, called to obey. That was a clear enough sign for me, but I waited until after Christmas before writing for application forms.

It was when the forms arrived and I was filling them out that I found I could stay for a maximum of three months. I wrote in the dates, "April 1 to June 30", and mailed the forms back to Patty Freeman, the co-coordinator of the Mission Builders at the time. Then I checked the calendar and realized that April 1 was Good Friday, and there would probably be little chance of a plane seat to Hawaii that weekend. However, I left it in the Lord's hands, and found that I didn't have to worry.

On March 5, Patty called me to say I had been accepted. She just had one question: "How soon can you be here?"

**Patty and Ken Freeman, Crossroads
Coordinators in 1994**

Then she explained that the staff librarian had been called home to Ohio to tend her sick mother. The Mission Builder who was helping in the library would be leaving on March 16, and there was nobody else with adequate skills to take charge of the library unless I could be there before then.

At the time, I was working in a restaurant, and had already arranged with my boss that I would leave at the end of March. However, I called my travel agent before I called my boss, to see if there were any available seats on a plane going to Hawaii in the next few days. She said there was a seat available on March 15, so I booked it. Then I called my boss and explained the whole situation. She was very understanding, and agreed that I could leave my job at the end of my shift on March 14.

On that day, after work, I took a bus to Victoria and stayed overnight in a hotel near the airport. I flew out on 15th to Honolulu, and then on to Kona. Patty's husband, Ken, met me off the plane, and took me to the Mission Builders' residence.

The complex where most of the Mission Builders and some of the staff lived was called *Hal'e Ola*. In the Hawaiian language, this means "House of Light". The compound held a group of eight two-storey buildings, each one having several bedrooms of various sizes. There was a bathroom with a shower on each floor, and laundry facilities in three of the buildings. One building also had a 'Common Room' where we could meet to celebrate birthdays, wedding anniversaries, and other special occasions.

To begin with, I shared a room with a Dutch lady who was due to leave about four days later. As a matter of fact, I had four different room-mates during that first three month stay, but none of them was there for more than a few days. I was quite happy to be on my own for most of the time, as my work took a lot of energy, especially before the staff librarian came back. It was also a struggle for me to acclimate to the heat and humidity.

I soon worked out a routine of waking about six o'clock, walking about a mile up the road to the main campus for breakfast, and starting work in the library about half past seven. The kitchen staff provided the Mission Builders with cold drinks and cookies at mid-morning every weekday. On Tuesday and Friday mornings, there was a worship service for everyone on the campus. It was held in the open-sided stone-built Pavilion at the centre of the grounds. These services were led by a group of students from a different school or college each week. One morning a week, all the Mission Builders came together for an hour of Bible study and intercession. [This has since been moved to a mid-week evening meeting in the *Hale Ola* Common Room.]

Almost every Friday evening, there was a campus meeting which was also open to the public. These meetings were held in the basketball court, if the weather was fine. If it rained, we all crowded into the Pavilion. The meetings always started with a time of worship, and featured a guest speaker. This was often someone who was teaching in one of the schools on campus that week.

I quickly learned my way around the campus, and figured out how the library was organized. The Mission Builder who was there when I arrived showed me where stocks of processing materials were kept, and how the shelves were arranged. At that time, the processing of new books and suitable donations was still done by hand on catalog cards with a typewriter. My shift ended at half-past four, and two student assistants looked after check-ins and check-outs and shelving returned books in the evenings.

The staff librarian, Betty Wagler, arrived back on campus on March 31. She had nursed her mother through a cardiac illness for two weeks, but her mother had subsequently died. It can't have been easy for her to come back to work so soon after such an experience, in a library where someone completely unknown to her had been in charge for two weeks. However, we soon found that we made a good team, and worked well together until mid-June.

There were several highlights, I recall from that first tour of duty with YWAM in Kona. One weekend, most of the Mission Builders took a trip up-Island to Hapuna Beach. This was a great place for surfing, when the tide was right. I didn't surf, but I did learn to use a "boogie-board"—at the age of fifty eight!—and I thoroughly enjoyed the experience.

One weekend, we visited the huge luxury Waikoloa Hilton Hotel. This was such a fantastic place, it is not easy to describe. The property had its own canal with free boat-rides for getting around. There was also a free monorail for the same purpose. There were two large landscaped swimming pools, and a dolphin pool. The public rooms were lavishly decorated with paintings, large Chinese vases, and bronze sculptures. There was a separate 'village' of luxury shops, and two golf courses. We were told that the price of a room started at $150 per night, with the Honeymoon Suite costing $1,000 or more.

After we ate lunch on the beach, some of us went swimming. I ended up swimming with a small group of sea turtles. That was something I shall never forget!

Another highlight of my first time in Kona was the luau at the King Kamehameha Hotel. The program was presented by a group of musicians and dancers called *Island Breeze*. This group had originated in the YWAM Music and

Worship school. As a Mission Builder, I was able to buy a ticket to the luau at a reduced price.

The guests assembled on the beach in front of the hotel, where greeters presented us with shell leis. Several members of Island Breeze were demonstrating native arts and crafts, and we had time to look around. One of the men climbed a coconut palm with a rope around his waist, cut loose a nut with his machete, and came down to show us how he opened it. Several of the women were demonstrating the hula, and then inviting visitors to join in. Their efforts caused considerable hilarity among the onlookers.

Just as the sun was setting, a canoe carrying a 'royal party' was rowed across the lagoon to the beach, where it was greeted by 'heralds' with conch-shell horns. They led us to an area where a whole pig had been roasted in an underground oven, and one of the group explained the process of preparing and cooking the meat, which took a whole day. After that demonstration, the pig was removed from the oven and taken to be carved as part of the banquet supper.

The eating area was under a huge tent, and there were several hundred guests. The food, which was set out buffet-style, included smoked salmon, poi, and some wonderful salads, as well as the roast pork, and traditional native desserts. After the meal, we were again entertained by Island Breeze, who performed traditional dances from each of the seven major Pacific Islands. It was quite a night!

Yet another highlight of that three month period was the time I went parasailing. Another Mission Builder friend and I took advantage of a special price-offer one weekend, and four other friends went with us. Two of them were there as spectators, and took photos of those of us who went for a ride in the sky.

I was a bit scared when I was first strapped into the harness, but I soon settled down. The boat was moving quite fast across the bay but it was so quiet and peaceful four hundred feet in the air. I could see fish, dolphins, and manta rays in the water, and had a great view across the land, too. I really didn't want to come down. I was very happy, later, when the photos came out well. Otherwise, my family would never have believed I could do something like that.

Chapter 4

MORE ABOUT YWAM AND ME

While I was working in the Kona library as a Mission Builder, I heard about a program, commonly called TESOL, or Teaching English to Speakers of Other Languages. As my professional background was mainly in teaching English, I thought that taking this course might be my next step. The good Lord thought otherwise. I registered and was accepted, but then could not raise the necessary fees.

I had been hearing about the courses known as D.T.S. or "Crossroads D.T.S." ever since I first went to Kona, but didn't fully understand at the time just what these courses were. (See Appendix). After asking some questions and becoming convinced that TESOL was not for me, I applied for the September Crossroads course. Robert York was the co-coordinator of Crossroads at that time, and he called me on my birthday in early June.

"Happy birthday, Kathy."

"Thanks but . . . why are you calling me?"

"I thought you'd like to know you've been accepted for Crossroads in September."

"Oh . . . thanks very much. I wasn't sure . . ."

"That's OK. We'll see you then."

So I went home that summer and returned in early September to work in the library for three weeks before the new course started.

On the first day of classes, I moved from *Hale Ola* onto the main campus, and into a room which I shared with two other ladies, both in their early sixties. Joy was English, from the Isle of Wight. She was the same age as my sister Joan, and a trained classical pianist like me. Barbara was from Los Angeles, and quite a different character. She just loved to shop! She went into town at least twice a week, and never came back without something new. We three were the oldest students in that Crossroads class, and we soon settled down together and became good friends.

My Crossroads roommate, Joy (2010 photo)

There were over seventy students in our class, singles, couples, and families with children. Seventeen of the students were from South Korea, and they were provided with headphones so they could listen to one of the two translators who took turns translating and explaining the lectures for them. The team of twelve staff was led by Rick Sorum, whose wife stayed in the background praying for any student or staff needs. There was also a Korean couple, Soon and Cheol. We students were encouraged to use Christian names for all the staff right from the start, but some of the Europeans and the Koreans found this difficult at first. It just wasn't part of their culture.

We had our own worship time in the auditorium on those mornings when there was no campus worship in the Pavilion. Different speakers, usually long-time staff members of YWAM, taught us for a week at a time. Topics included such subjects as "The Work of the Holy Spirit'; "The Armor of God"; and "Spiritual Warfare". Each student was assigned to a small group for an hour of intercession twice a week.

We were divided into different small groups where we discussed the week's teaching, prayed for personal needs, and told each other our life stories. I was delighted when I found that Patty Freeman had moved from being the Coordinator of Mission Builders to join the Crossroads staff that term. It turned out that she was to be my small group leader as well.

We had to keep a weekly journal, in a way which was totally new to me. I had a dream, during the first week of the course, about a Viking ship which was 'launching out into an unknown sea'. The dream was so vivid that that is what I called my journal entries. I drew a picture on the first page of my journal to illustrate what I meant. Our first assignment was to write a prayer to God, telling Him why we were taking the course, and reflecting upon what it might mean for us.

LAUNCHING

OUT

INTO

AN

UNKNOWN

SEA

First page of my Crossroads journal

Each week, we arranged our notes in three sections: things we already knew which had been confirmed through the teaching; ideas which were new and unfamiliar; and what might be the practical application for the teaching in our own lives. We also added two other items. One was about the speaker's teaching style and how we reacted to it. The other was a general comment about what kind of week we'd had.

There were three reports to write from books we chose from a recommended list, all by Christian authors. As a former teacher of English, I again found myself struggling to do this assignment in a way which was different from anything I had done or taught other students to do before. We were asked to pick out two or three principles of Christian life as illustrated by the book. Then we had to say how the author brought these principles to life, and provide Bible-related quotations to support our view. We also were asked to comment on how these Christian principles might affect our own lives.

One of the other things we did in the small group was to take turns in talking about our personal faith journey and why we had come to Crossroads.

We handed in our journals to Patty each Monday morning and sometimes, in our group meetings, she would comment generally on some of the things we wrote without revealing any particularly personal items.

We each met individually with Patty three times during the course. This was usually at lunch time. We discussed how we were feeling about the course in general, and about the teachings in particular. For me, this was the start of a long-lasting friendship, which still continues.

The small group also went out for some social time on three occasions during the term. Once we visited King's Mansion, which was located several miles from the main campus, and housed about twenty DTS students. Another time, we had a picnic on a local beach. The third time was for a final lunch together at the local pizza parlor.

Through the teaching, I was learning about aspects of faith which I hadn't encountered before. One week's teaching in particular brought me some brand new ideas. That was Dean Sherman's course on Spiritual Warfare. Having been brought up in the Methodist Church in England, and later being involved with the Anglican Church in Canada, this particular topic had never been mentioned. However, I learned just how important it is to do continual prayerful battle with the forces of evil which try to invade our lives. Dean gave us a thorough Biblical background for everything he taught, which I found impressive and convincing. I also wondered why I had not realized the necessity for this type of prayerful action before.

The whole Crossroads School went out together on a couple of weekends. On one of these occasions, we went to a local beach. Then we were divided into teams of eight students each, given a Bible text, and told to illustrate it in the sand. I don't remember exactly which text my team was given, but we were not judged as winners.

Another time, we traveled up-Island to Hapuna Beach Park. I had been there as a Mission Builder, and didn't like the strong waves so I didn't go into the water much that day.

Several of our visiting teachers offered to pray for us individually at the end of a session, usually on a Friday morning. It was during an individual intercession with Bernie Ogilvy that I was struck down in the spirit for the first time. In a private interview with Chris Harrison, another of our teachers, I was given three Scriptures to remember: Psalm 118, verses 5 to 9; Psalm 118, verses 13 to 15 and verse 17; and John 15, verses 2 to 5.

Patty Freeman went with me, and wrote down what Chris said:

"God is writing a new chapter in the book of your life. This will be a happy one for you."

Patty also wrote, "When you spoke of being lonely and not fitting in all your life, he prayed over you: "You brought her out of a lonely place. She will sense You have put her in a family. She will know how valuable she is to You. Release in her a new ministry and a new way of being used by You."

As he said this last thing, he was holding my hands, implying that they would be used by God in ministry. This was confirmed later in the course, and reminded me of the vision I'd had over twenty-five years earlier.

The various teachings during Crossroads opened up a whole new spiritual world for me. It changed my life to such an extent that I decided to be baptized before the course ended. Provision was made for this during each Crossroads course, and there were nine of us who took part from my class. We had a worship session around the campus swimming pool to start with, and then the nine of us stepped into the pool in turn. Rick, our leader, and David Rees-Thomas, a local pastor, immersed us, and David also prophesied over each of us as we came up out of the water.

I was given another 'word' about ministry, which Patty also wrote down for me:

"The Lord is giving you new strength so that you can bury any anxiety about the future.

We release Your Word in her heart and life, and we give thanks. These are hands that have served many. Bring into her life [other] lives to serve her. These hands will minister grace and the encouragement of God."

On the Saturday evening of the last weekend of term, the whole school went to the Royal Kona Hotel for a traditional 'Love Feast'. We had a wonderful meal, and then some of the students organized games, performed skits, and played musical items. My English room-mate, Joy, and I had been working on a version of Mozart's *Eine Kleine Nachtmusik,* arranged for four hands at one piano, and that was our contribution.

Chapter 5

OUTREACH BEGINS

During the term, students and staff had been praying for guidance about our Outreach. Eventually, it was decided that we should all go to the Philippines for the first half, and then some would go to Malaysia, and some to Thailand. We were given a deadline date for payment of the cost but, two days before that date, I was still $400 short. On one of those days, Joy found me in our room in tears.

"What on earth's the matter, Kathy?"

"Oh, Joy, I was so sure that the Lord wanted me to go on Outreach, but I still don't have enough money to pay my fees."

"How much do you need?"

"Four hundred dollars."

"Only $400? I can lend you that! You can pay me back after you return."

"How come? I thought you were going on Outreach as well?"

"I've decided not to do my Outreach this year, because I need to go home for a while. But I wanted to give the money I've saved up for my Outreach to someone who needs it. That seems to be you."

(By the way, Joy did do her Outreach the following year.)

Only three of our staff were going to supervise the Outreach. My small group leader, Patty, traveled to Manila with us. Her husband Ken was already there, and they were going to work with the people on Smoky Mountain, just outside the Philippine capital. YWAM has a base there, and the staff and students work among the outcasts who literally live on the mountain of garbage produced by the city of Manila.

Our school leader Rick divided us into traveling teams, each with a student leader who was responsible for keeping his/her team together in the various airports we would be traveling through, and who was also responsible for the passports of those students. This was a very sensible system, and worked beautifully. Not everyone in the class was able to go, but there were over eighty people in the group, including some families with children.

We actually left on Christmas Eve, about six in the evening. However, the staff had provided us with a delicious brunch earlier in the day. Then we had a worship service, and a Chinese gift exchange in the auditorium.

A Chinese gift exchange is so much fun, especially with a large group of people. In case you haven't taken part in one before, I'll try to explain: Each person buys a gift costing $5 or less, women buying gifts suitable for women, and men buying for men. These are put on a table in the middle of the room, with the men's gifts and the women's gifts in two different piles. One person is in charge, and assigns everyone a number. The person with #1 makes a choice from all the gifts, unwraps and displays it to everyone. Then #2 can choose a fresh gift from the table, or can take the gift which #1 has. That gives #1 another choice from the table. Each gift can only be exchanged a maximum of three times, so it is up to the person in charge to keep track. By the time the exchange reaches the last person, there will only be one gift left on the table. So that person has a choice between that gift and the one which #1 now has.

It took almost two hours to finish our Chinese gift exchange. However, by four o'clock, we were helping to load the trucks which would take our luggage to the airport. We had been limited to two suitcases each. With such a large group, there was a lot of luggage. My room-mate Barbara had quite a problem with this. Our favorite "shopaholic" had to ship a whole bundle of stuff home to California before she could leave on Outreach with only the two suitcases we were allowed to take.

Once the trucks were loaded, we all piled into the campus vans and other vehicles driven by volunteers, and set off for the airport. Our flight left at eight o'clock, and we flew first to Honolulu, and then to Seoul, Korea. However, Christmas Day itself was a non-event for us.

We had been in the air about two hours out of Honolulu when we heard the captain's voice:

"We have just crossed the International Date Line. It is now December 26."

However, we were to experience New Year's Day not once but twice in the coming weeks. That more than made up for missing Christmas Day.

When we arrived at the airport in Seoul, we had a ninety-minute break before our flight to Manila. Several of us were only too happy to lie on the floor and put our shoeless feet on the seats in the departure lounge. Our ankles were quite swollen after the eleven-hour flight from Honolulu. I even fell asleep for about half an hour, with my feet still propped up on the edge of a chair.

We were met in Manila by Ken (Freeman) and the Philippines' National YWAM Co-ordinator, Rodelio. They helped us through Customs and Immigration, then took us to the Pope Pius XII Retreat Center. It was quite a culture shock to feel the intense heat and humidity, as well as to see how many of the Filipinos lived. For one thing, the streets were six lanes wide, but that didn't stop someone from the outside lane making a left turn across all the other traffic at an intersection! One of the first things I saw while traveling from the airport to the city center was an ox-drawn cart piled high with hand-made baskets. You may be sure I took a photo of that!

Chapter 6

Philippine Experience

It was good to meet Ken at the Manila airport, and to have his help for the first day in Manila. Once we were settled into our rooms at Pope Pius Center, we all met in the Common Room where Rodelio gave us some orientation to the Philippine YWAM ministry in general. Then Rick told us about the seven locations where he wanted to send teams.

Our first ministry experience came the next day in a large park in central Manila. We held a short open-air worship session, and then divided into groups of three or four. We spent the next two hours strolling around the park, speaking to the people we met. We asked each person or group whether they knew Jesus. If the answer was "No," then we asked if they would like to learn about Him. Some of the answers were both interesting and enlightening. They ranged from "Non comprendo" ("I don't understand") to "I'd like to hear more, but I don't have time right now." A few people were really interested, and admitted they were already Christians, mostly Catholics. It was quite an eye-opening experience for me.

The next morning's worship session at the Pope Pius Center focused on the children in the group. Rick pointed out that they could be the open door to approaching adults with the Gospel message. Relatively few Filipinos had seen children with blue eyes and blond hair, and there were several in our group. After worship, we discussed our experiences in the park, and then Rick gave us our assignments.

The seven teams were again headed by student leaders, but different people from those who had shepherded us through the airports. The three staff people were going to circulate amongst the various locations. Different teams went to Agape Church near Angeles City, Baguio, Abra, Church of Hope in Manila, and downtown Angeles City. The team I was assigned to went to Olongapo City, about a five-hour bus ride from the capital. There were five other women on the team, one with her husband and two children. Only the team leader and I were Canadians; the others were either Danish or Norwegian.

As we traveled to Olongapo on our third full day in the Philippines, we passed several sites where we could see whole valleys full of l'haar (volcanic ash) from the recent eruption of Mount Pinatubo. We were told that people had found this volcanic ash useful for fertilizer in market gardens; for concrete block making in construction; and for paving roads when mixed with other substances.

We were very glad to arrive at the YWAM base in Olongapo, as some of the roads we had traveled were very rough indeed. The campus consisted of several two-storey buildings arranged around three sides of a courtyard. One block contained dormitories with bunk beds in most of the rooms. There were also several bathrooms and a sitting room in this block. The middle block was the working heart of the base. It housed a kitchen, dining-room, and work area. The third block was the leader's living quarters.

The leader of the base at that time was Asmund Orjasaeter, a Norwegian, and his Filipina wife, Melanie. They had a little girl, Marta, who celebrated her third birthday while we were there.

Olongapo is situated on Subic Bay, which used to be a major U.S. Naval Base. The navy had pulled out a few years before we arrived, and the city's economy was in very poor shape as a result.

The day after we arrived, Asmund took us on a tour of the city, using local 'jeepneys' for transport. These were converted American jeep-like vans which had metal roofs but open sides. They were painted different colors to indicate the route they usually traveled around the city. While we were looking around, Asmund explained that ministry out of the YWAM base consisted of working with the local children's orphanage; helping with a street kids' program sponsored by one of the local churches; visiting the local jail where men and women lived in neighboring but separate compounds; visiting a local mountain tribal village; and working with the girls in the 'red light' district.

This last was the main thrust of their ministry. Many of the girls who worked in the bars as waitresses and prostitutes did so in order to bring home good money. The YWAMers' job was to try and show them that there was a better way of life. If any of the girls consented to change their ways, they were brought to live on the base. If they had a low grade of education, they were sponsored through various schools in the area. They were also taught paper-making for greeting cards and stationery; dress-making and fancy embroidery; and other crafts by which they could make pocket money.

After the first couple of evenings on 'The Strip', I felt that I could serve better by baby-sitting for the Norwegian couple in our group. They were happy to be able to work together in the bars without having to worry about their two children. I was much more interested in the various aspects of children's ministry. I actually tried, later on, to arrange for the sponsorship of two children in the orphanage, but it didn't work out.

While we were in Olongapo, we had a choice of which church to attend on Sundays. A few of us went with some of the base staff to Calvary Chapel, which was where we also worked with the street kids. Most of us went with Asmund, Melanie and Marta to the I Care Chapel. I enjoyed the Pentecostal services very much, although they were very different from the church services I was accustomed to in Canada.

Asmund's deputy was a young man called Jun, (pronounced "yoon"). One Sunday, he took the Outreach team to a different Pentecostal church on the outskirts of Olongapo. Pastor Tony welcomed us, and we took over the service. There was a time of worship, and then we acted out a Christian mime-drama with commentary and translation. I had the privilege of telling the children's story, based on Psalm 23, and of expounding the same text to the congregation. As was expected, I also shared my personal testimony as part of the message. A young couple in the congregation had brought their new baby to be dedicated by the pastor. After the service, everybody went to that family's home for a buffet lunch.

While in the Philippines, we found that we could shop for groceries and toiletries at a very low price, compared to those in the U.S. This was especially true of hair and beauty treatments. Melanie showed us where we could have a shampoo, hot oil treatment, and a head and shoulders massage for about $2.50 U.S. We were somewhat surprised to find that many of the operators in these salons were gay men. It was just accepted as part of their culture.

One day we all climbed into a small praya at the Baretto landing on Subic Bay. These were the common fishing boats of the Filipino people. They consisted of a shallow curved hull, with a canvas covering supported by three or four very slim vertical logs on either side. On that day, we went across to a fishing village on one of the nearby islands, where we held a worship service in the little chapel. Then we visited some of the villagers who were sick, and prayed for them. If we had thought that the 'squatty potties' in some places we had visited were primitive, here there was only a four-foot-square hut with a hole in the floorboards for a toilet!

The very next day was a memorable one for all of us. Thirty-five people, including children, piled into one jeepney and traveled to the Bataan War Memorial. The last hill was so steep that some of us climbed out of the jeepney when we were only part of the way up, and hiked the rest of the way to the top. The huge hollow stone cross on the top of the hill is thirty stories high, and can be seen from far out at sea. Along with many of our group, I climbed the four hundred and four steps inside the stem of the cross and walked along the side arms. The walls of the horizontal part had floor to ceiling windows, and the view was absolutely breath-taking!

We had a picnic lunch, and then toured the underground museum. It was in these caves that American soldiers had 'holed up' during the Battle of Bataan which raged there in 1942. Now there are exhibits which tell the story of that battle, in which so many soldiers took their stand against the Japanese invaders and, unfortunately, lost.

On the way to Bataan that morning, we had seen many local people spreading their harvested rice along the sides of the road to dry in the sun. As we came back in the evening, they were gathering the rice into sacks to store it, or to sell at the market later.

A few days before we left Olongapo, Jun took us to another orphanage in the barrio (village) of Castillejos, called Jireh House. (The word 'jireh' is Hebrew for 'provider'.) This orphanage had been built with the help of the former U.S. naval personnel from Subic Bay and other Christian friends. The people at the orphanage had been through a very difficult time when Mount Pinatubo erupted, as they were located only about twenty kilometers away from the volcano. Christian friends again rallied around to clean up the mess then, and again when a nearby river flooded during the following especially heavy monsoon season.

After eating lunch at the orphanage the principal, Pastor Joel, drove us closer to the mountain. There was a huge dyke of l'haar, about ten feet high, stretching for many miles along one side of the road. We stopped and climbed it at one point, to see just how much damage had been created by the eruption. In one area we could see that a new lake had been formed, and that a river had been diverted almost a mile out of its former course.

There was an enormous open-pit copper mine not far from the base of the mountain, where we were given an explanation of the workings and shown the pit itself.

This was shaped like a bowl, about a mile wide and half a mile deep, with roadways carved along the sides in a spiral pattern. Trucks were working day and night, hauling the ore to a nearby smelter. These vehicles were also huge, with tires weighing up to one ton each. They could carry up to five tons of ore in each load. We were told that the mine also produced about two and a half tons of gold and silver each year, but would probably be worked out within another three or four years.

A YWAM team from Norway arrived at the Olongapo base with their leaders three days before we left. This meant that we had to reorganize our sleeping arrangements, but there was room for everybody. Life was certainly never boring at that base!

For a treat on our last day, we were taken to a small island owned by one of Asmund's friends. The boat trip took about three hours, and we saw some very varied plant-life along the way. There were mangrove swamps along the shore-line in many places, and we could see colorful parrots and other birds flitting in and out among the branches. There were rocky coral islets scattered here and there in the bay around which we traveled. Occasionally, we caught a glimpse of a native village with its huts made of native branches and thatch.

Once anchored just off the island, we were able to swim, dive off the boat, and picnic on the beach. I spoiled my own day by accidentally putting my right hand on a sea urchin just before lunch time, and getting a lot of its spines in my palm. I wasn't far from the boat at the time, but I was starting to black out with pain before I touched the side. Someone helped me on board, removed most of the spines, and gave me some limes. They told me to keep squeezing the juice onto the wounds. It really did help, but

I still became sleepy. So I took a nap before we started back to Olongapo.

The team traveled from Olongapo to Manila on January 21, picking up the two teams from Angeles City on the way. Three of the other teams had already arrived at Pope Pius Center by the time we reached it, and the seventh team came in shortly afterwards. The Center building had been painted while we were away, partly because Pope John Paul II was to visit Manila in February.

On the Sunday morning, we had a session of praise and worship, followed by intercession. Then we heard reports from each of the team leaders. That evening, we had a love-feast at the Holiday Inn, followed by a series of dramatic skits, one from each team. One couple had decided that they should go immediately to Japan, to help with the recovery from the recent Kobe earthquake. We prayed over that situation that evening, too.

Chapter 7

MINISTRY IN MALAYSIA

Before we started the second part of our Outreach, we spent a few days at the Peacehaven Retreat Center in the Genting Highlands near Kuala Lumpur. While we were there, Rick told us about the ministry opportunities available in Malaysia and Thailand. Four teams would be going to northern Thailand, and two teams would stay in Malaysia.

Everybody prayed about their personal choices that night, and we were given our assignments the next morning. I was asked to stay in Malaysia, as part of a team under the leadership of Lorne and Janet Gerber, a Canadian couple from Kelowna, B.C. The others on the team were an Indian couple and their young daughter, and an American couple.

The teams for Thailand set off at five o'clock on the morning of January 25, as their journey would take forty hours to complete. My team left soon after ten o'clock, to go by bus to Malacca. During our time in Malaysia, we also did ministry in Raub, the capital city of Kuala Lumpur, Ampang, Seramban, and Petaling Jaya.

The work here was very different from what we had done in the Philippines. We usually did some sight-seeing in the mornings, rested in the heat of the day, and collaborated with local Tamil Methodist or Presbyterian pastors in the evenings. We conducted Bible studies, prayer meetings, healing services, and regular Sunday services. We saw people delivered from demonic possession and generational bondage. Others were healed of a number of physical problems, and yet others were brought to belief in Christ.

For breakfast, we usually ate at the home of the head pastor in whatever town we were staying. Some of our other meals were eaten in the street markets and local restaurants. In a couple of places, love-feasts were prepared by the local church members in our honor. We often slept at the pastor's house, or in those of some of his congregation. This meant that we were not together as a team so much as we had been in the Philippines, but we held a group worship, Bible reading and intercession time each day that we weren't traveling from one place to another.

Of all the places in Malaysia that we visited, I liked Malacca best. It is a very old city, with Portuguese, British, Chinese, and native influences. The architecture is a real mixture, and I found it very interesting. Among other things, I discovered a naval museum, with sailing craft on display from all periods of the city's history.

Our stay in that country gave us a chance to sample a wide variety of the native foods, some of which I found quite intriguing in taste. Chinese and Indian foods and seafood predominate, but some restaurants also served Western dishes. I love Chinese food, anyway, and I was always eager to eat when we could have that. My stomach can't cope with curry or spicy food, no matter how mild, so when we went to an Indian restaurant, I wasn't so happy.

One dish I remember vividly, as it was put together right on the table in front of us. I think it was called 'satay', and it was prepared in a large pot of boiling water which had a steam vent in the middle. There were fresh crab legs, prawns, lovely white fish, and noodles. Each of these was added in turn, depending on the time it took to cook. When the mixture was ladled into our bowls, it smelled heavenly! We were told that the recipe was an ancient Portuguese one, which was only known to a few people. We felt very honored that one of the church elders had treated us to such a feast.

Kuala Lumpur itself is a fascinating city, very much a mixture of old and new, like Malacca. Some of the architecture, especially in the city center, is breaking new ground in design. Buildings such as the main railway station clearly show the Portuguese influence, while the building which houses the National Museum is a mixture of old and new. There is a Central Market where the stalls, although they are inside the building, are all draped with beautiful batik awnings.

Although Malaysia is eighty per cent Moslem, there is considerable religious tolerance. Buddhists are allowed to build their temples, and Anglicans, Methodists, and Presbyterians have their own churches.

While we were staying in Petaling Jaya, we enjoyed some of the Chinese New Year festivities, which lasted for several days. There were teams of lion dancers moving from street to street. As each one finished its performance, strings of fire-crackers were set off. When they finished sparking, dozens of people in fantastic costumes followed the lion dancers to the next stop. At night, there were hundreds of fireworks going off all over the city, which made it rather difficult to sleep.

On Saturday, February 18, all the YWAM teams returned to Peacehaven in the Genting Highlands for debriefing. The other Malaysian team was already there when my team arrived, but the teams from Thailand didn't arrive until the next day. We had a praise and worship session on the third day, and the team leaders each reported on their activities. The most remarkable report came from one of the teams who had gone to Chiang Rai in northern Thailand. They had stayed in a Christian orphanage which was managed by Rosa Martinez, one of our Crossroads student colleagues.

Some of the older children from the orphanage had gone with the team to a village in the mountains which had rarely seen white people, and never heard the Gospel message. With the help of the local pastor as interpreter, they held public worship services and also spoke about Jesus to individuals who showed an interest. By the third day, the village chief and his family, the shaman and five of his six sons, and most of the villagers had decided to become Christians.

The next day, we were told, the shaman's sixth son came to his father and asked to be taught all the spells and animistic practices of their former religion.

"I can't do that," the old man told his son. "When I accepted Jesus, all that was wiped from my memory."

What a story!

We left Genting on February 21, and traveled by bus to Singapore's Changi International Airport. It was still beautifully decorated after the recent Chinese New Year celebrations. We had an interesting few minutes there when the travel agent wanted to give us our tickets, without waiting for boarding passes. Our school leader Rick insisted we each have a boarding pass before he would surrender the tickets, and it was a good job that he did. We were six boarding passes (i.e. seats) short, but six of the Korean students agreed to go on a different plane which would land in Seoul a few minutes after ours.

Pastor and Mrs. Lee, two of our classmates who had not been on Outreach, met us in Seoul, together with our two Korean staff, Soon and Cheol. They had arranged for us to visit the Presbyterian church they usually attended when at home.

I had never seen such a church building! It was five stories high, with two more levels below ground. It was located on a major intersection in downtown Seoul, and had its own coffee-shop, gymnasium, library, and games room. There were three auditoriums of varying sizes, the largest of which could hold 2,700 people! They would have five services every Sunday: two in Korean; one in Japanese; and two in English.

Before going on to the airport, our bus driver took us on a tour of the city. One street which intrigued everyone was lined with shops displaying nothing but wedding outfits. Mr. & Mrs. Lee explained that although a wedding is one of the most important days in family life, many Koreans could not afford to buy special clothes. So there was a large local industry producing all the necessary items and renting them out. That was what all these stores were for, and the competition was keen to produce and display the most elegant outfits.

The flight from Seoul to Honolulu took about nine hours, and then we had to wait about ninety minutes for our connecting flight to Kona. For the next few days, we were housed in one of the resort hotels on the sea-front. What luxury after our recent living quarters! There were two swimming pools, and we had free passes for breakfast at the hotel's restaurant each day. It was heavenly!

We were not left entirely on our own, though. We had a final debriefing session at the Kona campus. We also visited the current Crossroads class, and several of our group spoke about their experiences.

There was also mail to collect, and one letter turned out to be crucial for me. Before we went on Outreach, Rick had interviewed each of us about what we wished to do afterwards. I had told him that I wished to stay in YWAM, and would like to get back into library work. He had referred me to Donna Jordan, who was leading a retreat on campus at the time.

She had two questions for me:

"What about coming back to Kona?"

"I'd love to do that, but the weather in July and August would be just too hot and humid for me."

"Then what about Australia?"

I started to laugh, and she asked why. I told her about Graham's and my abortive attempts in 1956 and 1959 to go to Australia and teach.

Donna chuckled, too, but then she said, "Maybe this is God's timing for you."

So I had written to Tom Hallas, the YWAM Director for all of Australasia. Now I was back from Outreach, and here was Tom's letter saying that they needed a librarian in Canberra. He enclosed staff application forms, which I filled out right away and mailed back to him, suggesting that I would sign on for two years.

On Friday, February 24th, the Outreach teams had a final meeting with Rick and the other Crossroads staff, which ended with Communion. I decided to stay at the hotel for an extra two days, and was able to keep the same room, beside one of the swimming pools. I rented a car and was able to help several of my friends with trips to the airport. I also met some Mission Builders who were friends from my first visit to Kona the year before, and spent part of one day with them.

Two days later, I was on my way to Seattle to spend a couple of days with a Crossroads friend who had not gone on Outreach. I took a Greyhound bus from there to Vancouver, and then went by bus and ferry to Nanaimo. My daughter and son-in-law, Elaine and Steve, met me there with their two children, and we had supper together. Then they drove me to Beach Acres, where I had to stay with another friend for a few days, as my cottage was in the rental pool until the end of March.

Chapter 8

AUSTRALIA AHEAD

Within two days, I had rented a car, reassured my family that I was safely home, and worked through a suggested "re-entry" process. The book recommended for all short-term and long-term returning YWAMers was Peter Jordan's book of that name, *Re-entry*. I had thought I would have no difficulty getting back into my regular life after Crossroads and Outreach, but Peter's book pointed out several items which I had not expected, and also suggested solutions.

Some of the questions he asked, and my responses to them were:

Why leave?

Because I believe God has called me to another area of ministry.

Do you have some 'hidden areas' in your life which need to be dealt with?

Unresolved conflicts with friends and family; sale of the house; what will the family think about my going to work in Australia?

What have you learned while on the mission field?

God is faithful!

I now recognize that I can deal with my physical limits. I can love unlovely children. I can tolerate travel under less than ideal conditions. I can find peace in the midst of spiritual struggles.

These are only a few of about fifty questions posed in the book, which also includes a personal "stress check". The book concludes with encouraging its readers to initiate meetings with those who have provided financial and prayer support. It also suggests ways in which we can be advocates of the YWAM mission purpose. These include staying informed, staying in touch, and keeping in prayer for those still actively involved with YWAM.

I put my cottage up for sale, and sat back to wait for results. Because Beach Acres was a resort with a strata council, owners were not allowed to live in their units for more than forty-six weeks a year. They must vacate for the other six weeks, not necessarily all at one time, and put their units in the rental pool. This, I came to understand, was the reason for the slow progress in the sale of my property. In fact, it took five and a half months, but other things were happening in the meantime.

I made three presentations about my YWAM experiences in the next few weeks. One was to my home congregation at St. Mark's. Another was to a United Church group in the area, and the third was to another Anglican Church. There were only a few people at each meeting, but the talks were well-received. In each case, I took my photo albums, my Crossroads journal, and other mementoes with me. I also spoke to the Outreach committee at St. Mark's about sponsoring two of the orphans in Olongapo.

In early May, Kerry Ward, the Registrar from Canberra, called to tell me I could proceed with my Australian visa application. In order to do this, I had to go to the Australian Consulate in Vancouver. When I arrived, I found that they had all the forms ready for me, but I needed a passport-type of photo, and a fee of $145 CAD. I didn't have a suitable photo with me, so they directed me to a one-hour photo shop just across the street. Once I had the picture and brought it to the Consulate office, I signed the necessary forms and paid the fee. A few weeks later, my visa arrived. I had to be in Australia no later than August 31. At the time, I thought there wouldn't be a problem, but getting there didn't prove so easy.

If I could have booked my air ticket more than fourteen days before my flight, it would have cost me about $1400. On a Sunday, thirteen days before I was due to leave, the house still had not sold, and I didn't have enough money in the bank for the price of the ticket. That was when a close friend called me.

She could tell I was really down, and asked specifically what was bothering me.

I told her, "I've been resting on the promise of our Crossroads text from First Thessalonians, chapter 5, verse 24: "The Lord is faithful and He will do it."

There was a slight pause, and then my friend said, "Yes, Kathy, but sometimes we have to take the first step."

That did it! On the Monday morning, I woke up praying for a miracle, but determined to do everything I could to bring one about.

I went to the travel agent to book my ticket to Canberra, and she told me, "You don't have to pay for this until the day you leave."

Although it would cost me $600 more because I was inside the fourteen-day prepayment period, I said to myself, "Thank you, Lord!"

Then I went to the bank and requested a loan of $3,000, based upon the probable sale of the house. The loans manager was also a Christian and, when I explained the situation, she stood with me. That afternoon, my realtor called with an offer on the house. While looking for one miracle, I had been granted three! By Thursday of that week, the bank loan had been approved. By the following Friday, the arrangements for the sale of the house were signed, sealed, and secure.

On August 30th, after a fifteen-hour flight via Honolulu and Sydney, I arrived in Canberra, Kerry met me at the airport and drove me to the base, which was housed in a former 1960's monastery.

The first three days were a blur, thanks not only to jet-lag, but also to crossing the International Date-line during the flight. However, I was able to join the Operations Staff for a prayer-walk around the central park on the second morning. I was also given a tour of the base, and had an interview with Tom Hallas. I hadn't realized until then that Tom was actually based in Canberra, although he was the Regional Director for all of YWAM in Australia, New Zealand, and the Pacific Islands.

Chapter 9

FIRST STAFF JOB

Once I had settled in, I found that not only was the Canberra YWAM base much different from the one in Kona, but it was a very different thing to be working on staff, rather than as a student or Mission Builder. I should have expected this but, for some reason, it only became clear when I experienced it.

I had my own room, for one thing. For another, I could choose whether I would eat in the dining-room, or make my own meals in the staff lounge upstairs. After talking to Tom, I was allowed to set my own hours, provided that I attended community worship on Monday mornings, and the Operations Staff meetings on Fridays. We agreed that a working time of thirty hours a week would be reasonable, and he allowed me to take Wednesday mornings off for a mid-week break.

The library at that time was located in a small former classroom on the north side of the inner courtyard. When I started, there were parallel rows of shelves with about 1800 books, some of them arranged in double rows with very little formal organization, even by subject. This meant that reference books, fiction and non-fiction books were all mixed up. There was a row of tables along one long wall with five computers on them. I also soon realized that many of the books which had Dewey Decimal numbers on their spines had been wrongly catalogued.

I started by separating out the reference books and arranging them on a set of shelves along the back wall. Big mistake! Two days later, the whole stack came tumbling down, creating a domino effect. When I came to work that morning, my first thought was that the library had been vandalized. Then one of the other staff ladies came by and told me she had been awakened about six o'clock that morning by the rumbling crash of the shelves going down. (She slept in a room immediately above the library.)

After that, I had all the shelves moved to the outer walls of the room, with the computer tables arranged in the middle. Then the maintenance man came in and secured adjoining shelves to each other, and all of them to the walls. This certainly made the room feel much less claustrophobic.

My work consisted of setting up a workable circulation (check in/out) system; an efficient way of regaining overdue books; computerizing the catalogue; correcting the cataloguing already in place where necessary; and writing a manual of procedures for both students and staff who might work in the library when I was not there.

At the time of my arrival in Canberra, one term was about to finish and a new one soon to start. In the last week of September, I learned what "Transition week" was all about. With no students and only a few staff on hand, the whole building was thoroughly cleaned, and furniture was moved from room to room to accommodate incoming students and staff. Breakfast that week consisted of cold cereals and toast. Lunch was sandwiches and fruit which we bagged up at breakfast time. Only the evening meal was cooked, and we all took turns helping to prepare it in groups of five or six each day.

Once the new term started, I was assigned two student aides who worked in the library on Monday to Friday for two hours between the end of classes and supper-time. On the first three days they were there, I stayed with them for part of the time, going over the manual and showing them the basics of circulation and shelving. I found that I had to make a few revisions in the manual but, once they had mastered the basics, I left them on their own.

In January, 1997, the library was moved to a corner room, which was about half as big again as the former one. With the purchase of more shelves, I was able to re-organize everything more efficiently. Both the students and I enjoyed the larger space, but it didn't stay unoccupied for long.

During my first three months in Canberra, I had been cataloguing the books from one of the smaller libraries on campus, as well as in the main one. When we moved the central library into the larger room, we decided to put the books from this smaller library in with the general collection. Then I identified each college's books with a differently colored spine sticker, just above the Dewey number label.

Soon after the New Year Murray Coleman, the campus architect, came to me with a draft of the plans for a major expansion of the library. We arranged to meet for lunch on Wednesdays to discuss them. We also started to research current library plans and new buildings at various University campuses in Britain and the United States.

We came up with what we thought was an ideal plan for the Canberra campus library, and he presented it to the Governing Board. We had worked it out so that it could be developed in several phases. We knew that the finances might not be available, even for Phase I until two years later, but we were very happy when the Board accepted the idea in principle.

At the same time, Murray was writing his doctoral thesis on library design as it has evolved since the building of the major libraries in Oxford and Cambridge. He needed a proofreader for his work and, knowing my background in teaching English, he asked me to help. He eventually received his Ph.D. in architecture about a year later, and cited my name among the acknowledgements when his thesis was published.

Chapter 10

AROUND THE WORLD
IN SEVENTY DAYS

I n early 1997, I consulted a travel agent about making a trip back to Canada later that year. She told me it would cost about $2800 for the round trip.

She also said, "If you could add another two hundred dollars, you could have a round-the-world ticket which would allow up to six stop-overs."

Of course I was interested, especially when she added, "You could pay for it in monthly installments, if you like."

So that's what I did.

On September 1, I took off from Canberra via Sydney to Singapore on the first leg of my tour. It was an extra 'plus' when I was upgraded to Business Class for the longer part of that journey. KLM really knows how to look after their Business Class passengers! It was the most comfortable airplane trip I have ever taken.

A Singapore Chinese lady met me at Changi airport. P.C. had worked on the Canberra base for one term while I was there, and we had become friends. She drove me to the apartment of a friend of hers, where I was to stay for three days. It was early evening when we arrived, but I was still on Canberra time. For me, it was half-past two in the morning but, as I'd slept for several hours on the plane, I wasn't ready to go to bed just then. We sat up chatting about YWAM and various other topics for several hours.

The next day, P.C. and I made a tour of the city. We visited the Cathedral, the Raffles Hotel, and the National Museum. In the evening, we went to the major shopping area on Orchard Road, and ate supper at a local restaurant. The next day, I was on my own, but P.C. had shown me the way to the local bus and train stations from the apartment, and had given me a street map of the city.

I took a train to Raffles Square, and then walked down to the river for a short cruise. I have found that cities look quite different when seen from the water, and Singapore was no exception. It was fascinating!

I spent the rest of the morning exploring the main shopping area, and then returned to the apartment for a rest after lunch. Although the heat and humidity were building up, I spent some time that afternoon wandering through the National Botanic Gardens.

About eight o'clock in the evening, I took a taxi back to Changi airport. My flight to Schipol (Amsterdam) International Airport took twelve and a half hours, but I slept for about four of them. I was headed for London Heathrow, where I arrived about eight in the morning, London time. I was drained, but I still had to travel to the British National

YWAM base at Harpenden in Hertfordshire. I finally arrived there three hours later, but it was eight in the evening by my body-clock. I was able to have a bath and a short sleep before supper.

I only stayed two nights, and seemed to spend a lot of time on the telephone. I was hoping to go from Harpenden to stay with a friend in Chesterfield, but that didn't work out. I also hoped I could visit the minister from the church I attended in Canberra, who was on a year's exchange in England, but that didn't work out either. Then I tried to call my family in Canada, but I had problems with that, too.

Finally, I was forced to rearrange my original plans altogether. As I love old cities, castles and cathedrals, and had never been to Chester before, that's where I went next. I spent four very happy and interesting days there. I visited the cathedral and toured *The Deva Experience*. This was an exhibition of the history of Chester, from pre-Roman times up to the present day. ("Deva" was the name given to the settlement by the Romans.) I also walked on the ancient walls. One day, I took a commentated bus tour and a river cruise, which gave me two different views of the city. I also took a day trip to Bangor in North Wales.

From Chester, I moved on to Hereford. I was curious to see this city, as my mother's family originally came from that area. I found that Hereford was another very old city with a very strong historical background. The highlight of my stay there was seeing the ancient 'chained library' in a building close to the Cathedral. I had never seen anything like it! There were several rooms full of huge oak shelving, filled with extremely old books, and each one securely chained to its shelf. I took some photographs so that I could show Murray when I returned to Canberra. Given the topic of his Ph.D. thesis, I knew that he would be as fascinated as I was.

Hereford also turned out to be a smaller city than I expected, which gave me an extra day to look around elsewhere. I decided to go to Shrewsbury, only a short train ride away. Once I arrived, I went to the Abbey and followed the 'Shrewsbury Quest', which will be familiar to readers of Ellis Peters' *Cadfael* novels. The Quest leads visitors through a number of rooms which illustrate different aspects of life in a monastery. There are also clues in each room which led those who were interested to the gradual solution to a murder mystery.

While I was in Shrewsbury, I also explored a 16th century merchant's house, and visited the Castle. Since Shrewsbury is located close to the border between England and Wales, it was heavily involved in the wars between the two countries in the Middle Ages. So it's not very surprising that the castle has been turned into a historical military museum.

I was back at the base in Harpenden by September 11, and was welcomed there by my Crossroads friend and room-mate Joy. She and I had arranged to spend a few days together, to save me the awkward journey to her home on the Isle of Wight. We went to Luton and St. Albans, an area where Joy had spent most of her life. We also took a day trip to London, which was slowly recovering from the recent death of Princess Diana. Joy and I both wanted to go to the famous Harrod's store, as neither of us had ever been there. I shall never forget the hundreds of bouquets of flowers in memoriam for Diana, which were spread along the sidewalk outside the famous store.

We both left Harpenden the next morning, Joy to return home, and I to visit my sister Joan in Plymouth. We had booked a taxi to take us to the station at seven a.m., but the driver was late. As a result, we had to wait for a later train, which was packed with commuters like the proverbial sardines in a can. We both managed to squeeze into a small space near one of the train doors, with our luggage sheltered between our feet. The crowds at King's Cross station in London were unbelievable! I had to drag my wheeled cases for what seemed like a mile to reach the Underground line I needed for my connection to Paddington station. Then I boarded the wrong train and had to make an unexpected change partway there.

I finally caught the train at Paddington with only three minutes to spare. Thankfully, I had reserved a seat, so I didn't have to search for an empty space. It turned out to be a 'slow' train (stopping at every station) until we reached Newton Abbott. Then it was 'semi-express' from there to Plymouth. I'd had no time to contact my sister before leaving London, but I called from the Plymouth station. Then I took a taxi to her house. I was exhausted so, after a cup of tea, I went to bed and slept for over two hours.

For the next few days, I had a fairly quiet but very enjoyable time with Joan and her husband Reg. Joan and I went shopping and swimming together, and we also had lunch in the city one day. Using my Brit-Rail travel pass, I went to see our cousin Babs in Kent for a couple of nights. I also went to Exeter one day and to Bristol another. Joan's three-year-old grand-daughter Katy spent a day with us, and we had a lot of fun with her. Katy is very bright and so lively that both Joan and Reg were quite tired by the time her mom Carole fetched her home.

On October 2, I caught the overnight 'sleeper' train to Waterloo, and went by underground from there to Heathrow airport. Because KLM does not fly from London to Vancouver directly, I had to go via Amsterdam again.

That turned out to be more of an adventure than I had bargained for. The plane to Vancouver was scheduled to leave Schipol at two-thirty p.m., and was first delayed by two hours. Then the passengers were told that we should not leave until the next day. A coach took us to a brand-new five-star hotel in The Hague, and the airline paid all our expenses.

The next day, we were reassigned to various flights. Four other people and I were put on a plane at two-thirty, just twenty-four hours later than originally scheduled. But we were 'bumped' to business class, with all the extra amenities. This was proving to be quite a trip, but it wasn't over yet!

I had arranged to stay with another YWAM friend, Vi, who lived a few miles outside Vancouver. However, since I arrived a full day later than expected, she could not pick me up at the airport, as we had hoped. I phoned another friend in North Vancouver, but she couldn't help me, either. I ended up booking into the downtown YWCA instead. By that time, I was just happy to have a bed to sleep in!

I had decided to visit my two older girls in Calgary before coming to Vancouver Island so, by ten o'clock the next morning, I was once more aboard a plane. Rose met me at the airport, and I stayed with her while I was in Calgary, visiting back and forth with Lynne and her family.

Some other YWAM friends came in one day from central Alberta, and we went out for lunch together. Lynne and I also took the children to a local wave-equipped swimming pool one morning, and we all enjoyed that. We had a family dinner at Lynne's house on the Sunday of Thanksgiving weekend. Then Rose and I took my grand-daughter Nicky to Heritage Park in south Calgary on the Monday. Neither Rose nor I had been there for several years, but what made this visit special was seeing the park through Nicky's eyes.

I moved back to Vancouver on October 16, and was finally able to contact Vi. We had breakfast together in the city, and then she drove me to the ferry dock.

It was as I was traveling towards Victoria on the ferry that I thought, "YES!!! THIS is HOME!!!"

I stayed with a family friend in Parksville, so that there wouldn't be any sibling rivalry. It was just great to connect with people I hadn't seen in over two years. I was able to visit with some of my family, as well as going to my 'home church' again. I went swimming several times at Beach Acres, and had supper one evening with Ernest, Guy, and Ernest's wife Micky. This was just the kind of visit I enjoyed, but I was looking forward to the rest of my tour also.

Before taking off again, I spent several days in Victoria with yet another YWAM friend. We had met in Canberra when Marie was doing her Crossroads there, and I had promised to go and see her when I came back to Canada again. We did a few touristy things I hadn't done before, including visits to Undersea World and Miniature World.

Undersea World is a building on the edge of Victoria Harbor, which contains a huge aquarium. Visitors walk down a clear Perspex tunnel under the waters of the harbor, and the aquarium itself is all around on three sides. You can see all the marine life, from sea anemones to sharks. While we were there, some of the staff were feeding the various fish. It was interesting to see the creatures' various reactions when they saw their 'lunch' arriving.

Miniature World is in a building along one side of the hostoric Empress Hotel. It contains dioramas of various phases of Canada's and British Columbia's history, as well as children's fairy stories and a miniature railway landscape.

When I returned to Vancouver a few days later, I went out to the Vancouver School of Theology to see if anyone

I knew from 1990 was still there. I was not really surprised when I didn't see a single familiar face.

From Vancouver, I flew to Honolulu on my way to Kona. I stayed at the same hotel where my class had stayed after Outreach. While I was in Kona, I walked up to the campus and visited with Patty Freeman and a few old friends. Two former colleagues from our time in Malaysia took me to the Friday night meeting on campus, and I met several other friends there.

On November 2, I flew back to Honolulu, where I had a few hours to sight-see before going on to Auckland, New Zealand, about midnight. Because the plane crossed the International Date Line, it was November 4 when I landed. I stayed in a Bed and Breakfast just outside the main shopping area, but it was on a bus route with frequent service to and from the city centre. I soon found the offices I needed for booking harbor ferry trips, a city bus tour, and the ferry to Waiheke Island. Altogether, I was able to make a pretty thorough survey of Auckland.

After three nights there, I moved on to Rotorua by inter-city bus. I had booked another Bed and Breakfast room there, and the owner met me at the bus depot and took me home with her. I found that she had provided me with a large L-shaped suite, with its own kitchen and bathroom. It was one of the nicest places I stayed on the whole trip.

While I was in Rotorua, I attended a traditional Maori dinner and concert. The meal reminded me of the luau I'd been to in Kona. The food included sweet potatoes, lamb, chicken, wild game, pork, beef, and potatoes. A large hole was dug in the ground, lined with hot stones, and covered with green vegetation. The food was laid on top, sprinkled with water, covered and left to cook for several hours. It was delicious!

I also went to the Maori Arts and Crafts Institute, visited the Rainbow Springs trout farm and nature sanctuary, and saw the famous geysers and hot springs.

I returned to Auckland by train, and stayed one night in the same Bed and Breakfast as before. The owner had to take me to the airport early, because he had other business appointments that day. I didn't mind at all, because I am an inveterate people-watcher. The plane took me to Sydney International airport, and I caught the courtesy shuttle-bus to the Domestic flight area. I called the Canberra campus from there, and two of the staff met me when I landed.

It had been quite an eye-opener of a tour, but I had really enjoyed it. Now I had five days to prepare for my move to Perth YWAM base in Western Australia.

Chapter 11

A DIFFERENT AUSSIE
EXPERIENCE

I t certainly felt weird to be in the Canberra campus
community but not of it. I was given a room in the
guest wing on the ground floor instead of my former
room on the staff level. I ate lunch and supper in the main
dining room, and used the guest wing kitchen to make my
own breakfasts. I was training someone else to take over my
job in the library, with the help of the manual I had written,
yet I was no longer the staff librarian. In some ways, I was
quite ready to take off on November 15 and start afresh in
a new location.

The move had come about through a number of
circumstances.

Almost exactly a year earlier, I had gone to Tom Hallas and told him, "I keep hearing the Name 'Perth' echoing through my head over and over, but I don't know why. There is a YWAM campus there, but do they have a library?"

Tom shook his head.

"No, they don't, but if they know someone is willing to go in and take hold . . . Would you like me to make some enquiries?"

We sat and prayed about it for a while, and then Tom said he would get in touch with Pete Brownhill, the Director of the Perth base. Pete and I played 'telephone tag' for several days in January before we finally connected. I was committed to work in Canberra until the end of August, and then was going to take a ten-week break for my round-the-world tour.

Pete said, "That's OK."

I told him about the generous work schedule which Canberra allowed me.

Pete said, "That's OK."

I said, "The earliest I could come would be November 15, and only for one year to start with."

Pete said, "That's OK."

So here I was, on November 15, 1997, heading for Perth in Western Australia, via Melbourne. I was met by one of the kindest people I have ever known, Sue Bowles. She was the assistant hospitality staffer for the base. Her husband John was a retired Anglican minister, and these two people were to become very good friends of mine.

At that time, the Perth base was split into three parts on neighboring streets. The hospitality office, kitchen and dining room, and some staff accommodations were on Hay Street in twin houses next door to each other. The offices and classrooms were in a four storey building two blocks away on Adelaide Terrace, which had only been leased to YWAM the previous January. Twenty staff and student apartments had been leased in a ten storey building on Clay Street, which was in between Hay Street and Adelaide Terrace. Some of the apartments, although quite small, had four to six students living and sleeping in them.

Sue showed me to a guest room in one of the Hay Street buildings for the weekend, as my apartment on Clay Street would not be available until the following Tuesday. It took me three days to recover from the three-hour time difference between Canberra and Perth, but I had found my way around the various base locations by then. I had also talked to Steve Warren, who would be my immediate boss.

A fairly large room in the Adelaide Terrace building had been designated for the library. The books, however, were scattered among the various classrooms. There were still no shelves to put the books on when I arrived, nor did the base have enough spare money to purchase any. However, Steve knew where most of the books were, and promised me some help to assemble them.

Within a few days, I had a desk and a computer, books were coming in, and I had started building a data base. I penciled Dewey numbers in the front of each book as I went through them, as I still had to order my processing supplies. Without any shelves, I laid the books on the floor in Dewey number order.

As the books were brought in boxes from the shelves in the classrooms, Steve had students move those shelves into the library. I could tell quite early on that there would not be enough space for all the items, as I was also receiving donations of books, audio and video tapes, and magazines. These came from various staff members, volunteer workers, and people in the local church community who had learned about the development of a formal campus library.

The problem of shelving was eventually solved by a very generous Norwegian couple who were leaving Perth to return home. They wanted to use some of their money to help the campus in whatever area it was needed most. They donated $1000 to purchase four sets of bookshelves from the local IKEA store. I had told Pete we would be 'pushing out the walls' by Christmas, and we almost were!

Meanwhile, I was getting used to a very different weekly routine from that in Canberra. There was a weekly staff meeting for worship, prayer, and teaching, as well as twice-weekly worship services for the whole campus. There were also once a week evening meetings open to the public, which were held at a nearby seniors' home. These were similar to the Friday evening meetings in Kona, with a worship session followed by a guest speaker. There were also twice a week small group meetings for prayer and intercession. These groups changed each term, so I came to know almost everyone on staff.

Another key item in the Perth program was outreach to the immediate area around the base. Mixed teams of staff and students went to various parts of the city and knocked on doors. We asked the people if we could come in and talk about Jesus for a few minutes. Some agreed and some didn't. It was most interesting for someone like me who had never done anything like that before.

I was also getting used to a very different climate. Canberra had four seasons, with summer in December, January and February. Perth has a Mediterranean climate, pretty warm all year 'round, and blazing hot in January and February. I found this 'high season' very difficult to cope with. I often could not sleep until about one o'clock in the morning because of the heat. I have found, during my life that, when I don't sleep well, I don't have the energy to work properly the next day.

The Perth base was working four terms a year, with a week of transition between each, just as Canberra had during the first year I was there. But in my second year in Canberra, I had become accustomed to working three terms with three weeks between for transition. Going back to the old system was not easy for me. I was so glad to have my Wednesday mornings free, and to take a break of several days every six weeks, regardless of the term schedule.

In the two years I was in Canberra, I had spent one Christmas holiday in Sydney and one in Melbourne. The year I was in Perth, I stayed on campus until after the New Year. We had hung stockings for everyone all around the main house on Hay Street for a week before Christmas. On Christmas morning, we had a Chinese auction with none of the gifts costing more than five dollars. Then we had a huge barbecue in the courtyard.

A couple of friends had offered me the use of their home in the suburbs for ten days early in January, and I was very happy to accept. Jean and Ray were going to visit their grandchildren, who lived in a beach community about fifty miles from Perth. I still had to go to work, but it was so nice to come back to a cool house in the evenings! I was actually able to survive the hottest January day at 42.6 degrees Celsius (shade temperature).

The new term started on January 12, and new students and staff were already coming and going when I returned to live on base. At the beginning of each new term, the leaders usually arranged for communal games in a nearby public park, as a means of bonding the community. One time, we went five-pin bowling instead, because rain and thunderstorms were forecast. I managed to crack a rib at the bowling lane. The doctor couldn't do much for me except prescribe pain-killers and rest. However, when I went to my usual mid-week Communion at the Cathedral, Father Ken prayed for me, and I was healed.

In late May, I was very happy to greet my English friend Joy, who came to work in the hospitality department. She stayed in my apartment for a few days, but eventually rented her own apartment in the city. We were in a term break when Joy arrived, and I was on my way to a holiday in Kalgoorlie, but Joy had another friend in Perth, so she wasn't entirely on her own.

In mid-July, I received a call from Alan May, the head of academic studies back in Canberra. He wanted to know whether I would consider returning to Canberra, if Pete would release me before my twelve months' contract ended. I had to put him off for a couple of days, as I had been talking to the YWAM people in Adelaide about going there to organize a library for them.

With a lot of prayerful consideration, I was soon able to call Alan and say that I would return to Canberra in early September. I had told the people in Adelaide that I didn't really have the energy needed to start a library from scratch again, as I had done in Perth. I also had to consider that one of the main reasons for Alan's asking me to return to Canberra was that the plans Murray and I had made for the library expansion were finally coming to fruition.

Chapter 12

Holidays "Down Under"

Since I was over 8,000 miles from home, from the beginning of my time in Australia I determined that I would try and see as much of the country as I could. For the first Christmas, I thought that Sydney was the obvious choice. I could combine a different kind of Christmas holiday with a business trip to the Koorong bookstore, which was our major Australian Christian book supplier.

There were two different city bus tours on offer in Sydney, and I took advantage of both. I also went to Manley Beach on the north shore, visited Darling Harbor, and walked around 'The Rocks', which is the oldest part of the former convict settlement. I took a coach tour through the Blue Mountains, and a cruise on Jervis Bay to watch dolphins. On Christmas Eve, I went to a carol service at

St. Andrew's Cathedral and, on Christmas Day, I enjoyed a special meal at a local hotel.

I also went out to the nearby town of Parramatta, and strolled around its historic sites. One of the most interesting of those was Elizabeth Farm. This was built for John and Elizabeth MacArthur in 1793, and is the oldest surviving building in Australia. The MacArthurs were the pioneers of the Aussie sheep industry, and their home became a center for the social, political and cultural happenings of the day.

The house was originally built as a typical English country cottage. In order to cope with the heat of the Australian summers, the verandahs were later extended, and the building became a prototype Australian country home. Today, it contains copies of the furniture and furnishings which would be found in an early nineteenth century home, and it is surrounded by a re-created 1830's garden.

Celebrating Christmas in 30 degree heat was very different for me, but I enjoyed this one very much.

The second Christmas, I went to Melbourne. It was a very different kind of city from Sydney. It reminded me of the difference between Vancouver and Victoria in British Columbia, or between Edmonton and Calgary in Alberta.

Melbourne is another historic city, but not as old-established as Sydney. There was a beautiful botanic garden, and an old jail where the famous rustler Ned Kelly had been hanged over a hundred years ago. I saw some lovely countryside around the city, especially up in the Dandenong Hills. I took a 'puffing Billy' tour up there, traveling on a train with an old-fashioned steam engine. It was made up of wooden carriages with wooden seats and wide open window spaces. I also visited a local winery and restaurant on another tour. This place was remarkable for its chandelier in the dining-room, which was made up of empty wine bottles. Melbourne is located on the Swan River, but is not far from the ocean at the little town of St. Kilda. I took the local train there a couple of times, so that I could walk on the beach. This was one activity I missed while in Canberra as that city is about a hundred miles from the coast.

On another trip I made to the Melbourne area, I went to Ballarat to see how the old-time gold miners had lived and worked. While I was there, some local actors put on an elopement drama right in the middle of the main street. I had a chance to pan for gold which had been seeded in the creek, but I didn't find any.

During one of the term breaks while I was in Canberra, I visited the Gold Coast area of southern Queensland. There were four large theme parks to enjoy, and I also took a boat cruise over to Stradbroke Island. I spent one day in Brisbane, but the weather was too hot to walk far. I was quite happy to stay close to my hotel and its swimming pool.

On two different occasions while I was in Oz, I went to Tasmania. I made one trip by plane via Melbourne to Hobart, where I joined a five-day coach tour. Among other things, we visited a Cadbury's chocolate factory, the historic town of Richmond, the open-cast lead mine at Queenstown, and the Cradle Mountain National Park. We finished the tour on the north coast of that island state, with brief visits to Stanley, Devonport, and Launceston.

The second time I visited Tasmania, I went to Melbourne by air, than caught the car ferry to Devonport, and stayed in a bed-and-breakfast in Launceston. From there, I made a coach tour of the Tasman peninsula. This included a visit to the old logging settlement of Bushmill, and also to the historic penitentiary at Port Arthur. On this trip, I also went across to the southwest side of 'Tassie', and stayed in Straphang for a few days. This gave me a chance to make another boat cruise up the Gordon River, and to visit the former convict jail on Sara Island.

At one point while I was working in Perth, I traveled by coach, first of all going south through the Stirling Ranges to Albany, which had been the first British settlement in Western Australia. From there, we went to Pemberton and visited a still-active logging mill. We saw some of the old-growth forest where they obtained their lumber. Part of this forest is protected as a Nature Reserve, and we toured it by a steel walkway suspended in the canopy about thirty feet above the ground. The coach took us further south from there, stopping briefly at the southernmost point of the continent where the Indian and Southern Oceans meet at Cape Leeuwin.

Another adventure took me on the famous *Indian Pacific* train to Kalgoorlie, which used to be the center of the Australian gold-mining trade. In the nineteenth century, the gold was transported from the mines in the outlying areas to the town by camel trains. In order to cope with these, the streets of Kalgoorlie were built wide enough so that a camel train could easily do a 180 degree turn.

The tour guide and I had the mini-coach to ourselves when we went to Coolgardie the next day. We visited a camel farm which was now mostly a tourist attraction. The guide also showed me around the local gold-mining museum. On another day, I took a tour out to the Hannah Mine, which is one of the largest open-cast gold mines in the world, South Africa notwithstanding.

On another holiday out of Perth, I went north to Kalbarri. The museum there had some very rare wooden Native stick figures, only one hundred of which had ever been made. It also had one of the largest bottle collections I had ever seen. They were of all shapes and sizes, ranged on the shelves which filled the walls of a fair-sized room. The Murchison River region near Kalbarri had some fantastic sandstone rock formations, and there were others along the coast outside the town.

One day, I took a coach tour to Monkey Mia, and watched some of the tourists feeding the wild dolphins which made a habit of coming inshore each day at the same time. That made for some pleasant memories! On the way back, the coach stopped briefly for us to walk on a beach composed of nothing but millions of hard-packed tiny white pearly shells, with not a grain of sand in sight. That was quite an experience, too.

York was another historic town somewhat inland from the west coast. I took one of my four-day breaks there. It had been developed in the late 1800's, and was very interesting for a history buff like me. I saw a museum there with the original telephone exchange on exhibit. One old mill building had been converted for the making and sale of hand-tooled wooden furniture, including some beautiful Scandinavian-style sleigh-beds.

There were so many places, so different from what I was used to seeing in Canada, or in England when I visited. Australia was like a different world, and I was fascinated by its variety.

Chapter 13

Return and Renovation

B y early September 1998, I was on my way back to Canberra. I had amassed some Frequent Flyer points, which meant I could make a stop-over in Adelaide for a few days. Then I only had to pay for my flight from Adelaide to Canberra. As the capital of South Australia, Adelaide in one beautiful city!

One very enjoyable trip I made into the surrounding countryside took me to Hahndorf in the southern Highlands. This place was originally settled by German immigrants in the 19th century, and still retained much of its old-world charm. Many of the buildings were German or Austrian in design, and many of the people still carried on their traditional trades. One of the major occupations was wood-carving.

I also took a full-day coach tour, first through the Adelaide Hills, and then on a paddle-wheel boat on the Murray River. The guide took us to a nature park, where there were many native animals (including crocodiles!) and a Butterfly World exhibit. From there, we went to a special farm where emus were being raised. The farm had a shop for selling many different products, from emu skins and feathers, to the large emu eggs.

From Adelaide, I traveled business-class by air to Melbourne, thanks to my Frequent Flyer points, and then on to Canberra. Two of the YWAM staff were waiting to meet me, and helped me settle in my new room on the staff corridor. The next day was a Sunday, which enabled me to work my way back into the community in stages.

On the Monday, I was still not really back to work. Murray, the architect, showed me the final plans for the first phase of the expanded library, and how the computer lab would be combined with it to form a multi-level Learning Resource Center for the campus.

In light of this, I was asked to join the newly-formed Academic Affairs committee. I saw this as a recognition that the caretaker of all the resource materials on campus was now in a second-level management position. It gave me a bit more clout with the leadership, who now seemed more willing to consider my suggestions and act on them.

From that time on, I was not only doing LRC orientation sessions with each new intake of students on campus, but also helping the students in the Christian school to locate and use various types of resources. I also started to take in and catalog the research papers required for some of the courses we offered, once they had been graded by each particular school's staff.

Expansion was in the air, but we had to wait until early 1999 to actually start work. The main factor which delayed the start was the fact that many Mission Builders (volunteer workers) were not available until mid-January. When they came, they started by resurfacing the verandah outside the library, and varnishing the window-sills inside and out.

Once the guys were ready to start work on the actual rooms, I organized the removal of the books and computers to a much smaller room, which had formerly been the upper-grades classroom for the Christian school. Greg, the school principal, had one crew emptying shelves in the "old" room, and moving both shelves and books. I had another group setting up and re-shelving the materials in the new room. The main problem was how to persuade people who knew little or nothing about library shelf organization to keep the books in Dewey number order as they placed them.

Fortunately, there were about four sets of shelves in the room before we started, but books were being shuttled to the temporary room faster than my helpers could shelve them. How we managed to fit everything in, I'm not sure. There was barely three feet of space between the rows of shelves, and five computers were crammed onto tables around the walls of the small teacher's office in one corner of the space. There were about twenty very tired people by the end of that day.

**Canberra extended library with
"Wisdom Wall"**

In the midst of all this, a new term was starting, and I had to arrange orientation sessions. Since it took me a good two weeks to put everything where I needed it, these sessions were somewhat delayed. It was also high summer in Oz, and I was sleeping very poorly because of the heat.

After a lot of discussion, research and prayer, Murray and I decided to make one end wall of the expended library into what we called the "Wisdom Wall". The passage we decided to use was from the Bible, Proverbs Chapter 1, verses one to seven. It would be one of the last things put into the library, but it would give everyone a goal to work for. We announced our decision at a Monday morning worship session, and received a round of applause. Students and staff were encouraged to buy one or more four-inch brass letter(s) each, and thus have a personal share in the expanded Learning Resource Center.

After all the work and worry of moving, it was just great to be able to spend a few days down on the coast relaxing.

I hadn't realized how much I had missed being near the sea until I went to Ulladulla.

When I returned to the campus, I found that the volunteer workers had removed the original floors, ceilings, and electrical fittings in the first three rooms on the north verandah. Then the first connecting wall came down, soon followed by the second one.

Although I didn't do any of this physical work, a friend took a fun-photo of me standing next to a wall with a sledge-hammer in my hands. The next stage was to erect steel beams to support the ceiling where the walls had been.

By the last week of March, Murray and I were checking out second-hand furniture suppliers, looking for suitable office-type furniture. Three weeks later, we were choosing patterns and fabrics for the drapes. New energy-saving lights had been installed in the new ceilings, and they were working fine. It really made a difference!

Painting the ceilings and then the walls had started by mid-April. Then we had problems with people who had no real authority wanting a part in the decision about material for the drapes. We finally worked that through, but ordering the material was set back at least two weeks until proper lines of authority had been established. This delay meant that the sewing was also delayed, but finally everything was ready for re-stocking the shelves and returning the computers to their own section of the much-enlarged room.

We had arranged an area with lounge chairs around a coffee table where people could read magazines and chat quietly. We also had a special children's area close to where the Junior and Easy Fiction books were shelved. We called this, "Kids' Korner". My office area was in a central location, midway between the book shelves and the computer tables. It was also close to the file cabinets of vertical files and the specially-built tables with drawers full of audio-tapes. Another area housed shelves of video materials, with head-phones available for private listening.

In the first week of May, we started to move books and book shelves out of their temporary quarters into the new Learning Resource Center. A new term started on May 17, and I had the help I needed to move the last items from the temporary classroom. On May 24th, after the usual worship meeting, all the staff and students were invited to walk through the new LRC and pray over it.

It was June 4th before the material for the drapes arrived, and two of the ladies on staff were able to set up patterns for sewing. A third lady, off-campus, did all the actual stitching for us—a huge job for which we were very grateful.

By this time, all the stress of the upset was affecting me physically, and my doctor agreed that perhaps I should seriously consider returning home once the new LRC was officially opened. In the next few weeks, I spoke often with Alan May, the head of academics, with several of the leadership staff, and with my minister at the nearby Anglican Church. No definite decision was made for some time, but it wasn't long before I booked an air ticket to Vancouver via Tokyo, for August 22nd. I had been feeling subconsciously that my time in Canberra might never end, but now I was quite relieved.

By early July, Murray and I were ready to start setting the Wisdom Wall up. We were still short of funds to complete it, but we appealed to the community again on a Monday morning, and more donations trickled in. Several pairs of drapes had been sewn and hung by this time, and I was pressing Tom Hallas for a definite date for the official opening. I had written a short summary of the whole project, which was based upon the notes I'd kept, and the photos I'd taken. This I submitted to Alan May, for inclusion on the program for the official opening ceremony. This was finally arranged for Wednesday, July 21st.

The Monday and Tuesday of that week were hectic! I was able to obtain some ribbon suitable for cutting from the housekeeping department. I made another appeal for donations towards the Wisdom Wall on the Monday morning. The lettering on the wall was completed on Monday afternoon, even though all the letters were not paid for.

On Tuesday, the campus secretary finished a special sign for the main library door, and I arranged with Tom's wife to have refreshments served after the ceremony.

Finally, it was four o'clock on Wednesday, and most of the staff and students were gathered on the grass outside the LRC. There were a few short speeches and a dedication prayer. I was presented with a bouquet of flowers. Then the ribbon was cut. People streamed into the new facility, and made some very complimentary remarks while sharing the refreshments we had provided.

At last, I could truly relax. On the Friday of that week, I made my final trip outside of New South Wales. I went to visit my friend Anne Grimmond, whom I had met when she was leading a Crossroads school on campus two years earlier. She lived in Rockhampton, west of Brisbane, which was a very attractive town. We visited with some of Anne's family on the Saturday, went to church on Sunday, and toured some of the local beauty spots on Monday. I returned to Canberra on July 31st, after a very relaxing "time out".

A young lady named Bonnie was on campus when I arrived. She was going to take over the management of the LRC after I left, and I had just three weeks to teach her what she needed to know. I soon found that she was a fast learner, and I felt confident that she could do the job.

The special table with drawers for the audio tapes had been delivered while I was away. Part of my time that week was spent in making sure the information about the tapes was accurate and complete on the computer and the printout. Another term was over, and it was the last one I would see in Australia. I was getting terribly tired by that time, but I managed to keep busy for the last few days. As a memento, I bought a print of the Aboriginal painting *Shaman*, to be hung in the LRC.

The Operations staff gave me a farewell tea in the board room one morning shortly before I left, with various people speaking affirmations for me and praying for me as well. I had one final very nice memory to take away with me, as a Korean student couple was married in the campus courtyard on the last Saturday I was there. The wedding was totally bilingual, and very traditional in the Korean way.

All too soon, it was August 22nd and I was on my way to the Canberra airport one last time. Jacob, one of our Korean staff, and four of his students were traveling to Sydney on the same plane. I was happy to have his help in finding the right line-up in the Sydney airport for the plane to Tokyo. It took nine hours for that leg of the journey, and nine hours from Tokyo to Vancouver.

This time, my Mission Builder friend Vi was waiting for me, and I went to stay with her at her home just outside Vancouver for three days. I finally arrived in Nanaimo by ferry, and my daughter Elaine and her husband Steve and the children were there to meet me. They took me to my friend Lilian's house in Parksville, where I had arranged to stay until I found a place of my own. It took me quite a while to realize that I WAS home, and did not have to go to work or do anything I did not feel like doing. It was such a relief!

Take the Wings 4

THE LAST TEN YEARS

Note: For those of you who don't know, this memoir was first published in 2006. I continue now with material from the last chapter of that book, with up-dates to 2012.

Chapter 1

BACK HOME

A number of things happened during the five years between my return from Australia and the original publication of this memoir.

When I returned from Australia in August 1999, I stayed for a time with a friend in Parksville while looking around for a place to live. I checked out a number of places, and finally settled on a furnished duplex also in Parksville. I was working part-time at Elaine and Steve's store, which sold vacuums and kitchen appliances and parts.

While I was there, my friend from the local Emergency Social Services office, Judi van Swieten met another young lady named Lynda who was interested in YWAM. The three of us met for coffee one morning, and I met Lynda again a few days later. By that time, she was headed for a Crossroads

D.T.S. in Canberra, and we kept in touch for several years. She later became a missionary in south-east Asia.

I had taken a one-year lease on the house, but the owner decided to come back after ten months, so I was once again looking for a place to live. I found one closer to town, and once more had the joy of working in a garden in my spare time.

During this time, I was doing volunteer work with the local Emergency Social Services office, working with Judi, who was the director for our area. I was also playing the organ occasionally for the family service at my "home" church, St. Mark's. Some Sundays, I played at another Anglican church in the area. I was busy!

I hadn't forgotten my time in Kona by any means, and was working on returning there for a six-month stint. Everything was cleared by late September 2000, and Lynda agreed to house-sit for me.

I made my way to Vancouver on September 23, and stayed with Judi, who had recently moved to the University of British Columbia to become the head of ESS for the campus. The next morning, I caught a bus going to Seattle, but ran into a problem when we crossed the border.

The officer asked me where I was headed and how long I was planning to stay.

I told him I was going to the YWAM base in Kona to work for six months less one day, but that I would be working as a volunteer. He made me go over this information twice, and also asked if I had a letter from Kona.

"No, I don't. I asked for one, but haven't received it yet."

"I don't know what to do with you," he replied, stamped my passport, and said, "Get out of here!"

I thanked him and returned to the bus.

We were further slowed down on the way to Seattle by an accident near Everett involving a large truck, and arrived almost an hour late into Seattle. Fortunately, I had booked a room in a hotel near the airport for that night, so it didn't matter all that much.

The next day, I flew via Honolulu to Kona, and the new head librarian Madge Bridges met me there. I had a single room at *Hale Ola*, and was soon settled in. There were several Mission Builders and staff whom I had met when I was in Kona before, and that helped me this time.

I soon settled into a routine of walking to the campus for breakfast, and then working until about 2 p.m. each weekday. It was very different being on staff in the place where I had previously been both a Mission Builder and a student. My main job was to fine-tune the items on the computer data-base, not all of which were complete, or entered into the records in the same way. I also handled any donated items, and books which were waiting to be catalogued.

We also moved the library from one office to another while I was there. This involved packing, labeling and moving literally dozens of boxes of video tapes, as well as books and magazines, and then unpacking and deciding where everything was going to go in the new room. One advantage was that there was a second floor to the new quarters, and we were promised that air-conditioning was going to be installed. What a relief! Of course, moving everything and re-shelving the books also meant that I had to check them on the computer as they were unpacked. I found quite a few errors but, since nothing was shelved without a correct computer entry, I soon figured out where the mistakes were and put them right.

It was good to be able to go to Calvary Community Church on Sundays again, with David Rees-Jones as pastor. He remembered me from my baptism on campus several years before, and welcomed me back with a big hug.

While I was in Kona this time, I joined a group of students and staff who worked a water station on the marathon part of the International Iron Man competition in October. One of our own staff was taking part, and we saw him run in both directions. It was interesting to see the runners from many different countries, and to know how exhausted they must be by the time they came past our station with only a couple more miles to go.

On November 2, the weather turned very stormy. The rain was so heavy that it affected our electrical power during the night. We heard that the town of Hilo on the north coast had twenty-two inches of rain in twenty-four hours! It seems that there was a cyclone-type weather system "stuck" over Hawaii Island, and things would not clear until at least the next day. Madge decided to avoid having the lights go out and the computer systems go down, and closed the library about 10:30 a.m. By 1:30 p.m., the storm had passed over us, and everything was back to normal the next day.

Later in November, I went to a Renewal conference on campus, led by Peter and Donna Jordan. The music group "Island Breeze" gave us a Hawaiian welcome, complete with leis. Dan Sneed, a YWAM teacher led the teaching, based on various Bible passages. We also heard the latest news from the YWAM "Mercy Ships", and enjoyed a luau at the King Kamehameha Hotel. We finished with the usual Love Feast on Friday evening. Those attending spoke of expectations fulfilled in various ways, and we all joined in the final Communion service.

During the Christmas break, I spent a few days on the island of Maui. The highlight of that trip was a dawn visit to the extinct volcano *Haleakela*. It meant getting up in time to catch the coach at 4 a.m., but I made it. It was quite something to watch the sun rise over the caldera, and the sky colors were wonderful. The other major thing I did was to visit Lahaina on the other side of the island from where I was staying. I explored the old "Whalers' Village" and rode on the "sugar-cane train". I also made sure I took photos of the banyan tree in Lahaina which spreads out over a whole block of the downtown with its hundreds of branches and roots.

By late March, I was on my way home via Honolulu and Seattle. I had decided to use the shuttle coach from Seattle to Vancouver, as I had done on my way south. This time, I went through customs at the border with no problems.

I had arranged to meet Guy at the Vancouver airport, which was one of the regular stops on the coach's schedule. But Guy didn't come, and it took me some time to find out that Elaine was coming instead. She was meeting her daughter Lynne as she returned from a visit to Israel with the Youth group from their church. What I hadn't bargained for was the seven hour wait between my coach arriving and Lynne's plane landing. I was so grateful to be able to finally rest on the ferry to Nanaimo, and to have Steve meet us and take me to their house. It was 11 p.m. when we arrived, and I had forgotten to phone my house-sitter, and let her know I wouldn't be home until the next day. I was just exhausted!

I also made one trip to visit family and friends in England, which went much more smoothly than the one I made in 1997. This time, I made four stops, and in each place, except at my sister's home, I was concentrating on doing genealogy research. This had become a passion of mine when I was in Canberra the first time, with access to the National Library of Australia's collection of British records of births, marriages and deaths. Now I have no less than five binders of material. There are three for my grandmother's side of the family and their ancestors, one for my mother's people, and one for my husband's family. I also have one each for more details about the recent generations of these people, and for historical background material and photographs on the places where they lived.

I have also become interested in creative writing. Soon after I moved to Qualicum, I joined a writers' group which met twice a month. I really enjoyed the sessions, and especially the challenge of writing to a different theme for each meeting.

When I came home from Kona in March 2000, I went to see the minister at the Anglican church I used to attend.

I told him, "You know, Andrew, after six months of YWAM-style worship, I don't fit into a little Anglican box any more."

As a former YWAMer himself, Andrew knew where I was coming from, and released me to find another church home. I am now part of an evangelical congregation which meets just outside Qualicum, where I feel much more free to express myself in worship. I belong to a very caring mid-week home group and was, for some time, a member of the prayer chain. Intercession is a major part of this congregation, as is healing ministry, and I am involved in both.

In 2003, I had the privilege of traveling to Vancouver and meeting with my former Australian boss, Tom Hallas. We had lunch together at the home of the Vancouver YWAM leader. Then we were able to spend over an hour catching up with the past four years' happenings in both our lives.

On the way back to where I was staying with a friend, Tom happened to say, "You know, we could still use you back in Canberra."

I jokingly replied, "I'll come any time if you'll pay my airfare."

What a surprise when Tom cracked back, "You know, that may not be entirely impossible."

So far, it hasn't happened, but who knows? Actually, I don't think I could cope with the long flight from here to Canberra, much less the full-time work in the library. I just don't have the energy I used to have.

Chapter 2

A Home of My Own

I t took me two years to find the apartment I now live in, but I am so blessed to have it. I moved in, in early May 2001. It is located in a sixplex, which was built in 1979, right in the centre of Qualicum Beach on Vancouver Island, a beautiful small town which retains its village atmosphere. The building contains four two-bedroom apartments and two single-bedroom ones. The apartment I moved into first had just one bedroom, a small kitchen, a larger living area, and a bathroom, but there was quite a bit of storage space. The kitchen window looked out on the downstairs unit's patio garden and the front window faced the street.

I stayed there for about fifteen months, and then had the opportunity to move across the hall into a two-bedroom unit. I've been there ever since. I had told some of my church friends what was happening, and was promised some help.

The former occupant moved out on the Tuesday, and I was able to pack boxes and transfer them to the new place ahead of time. On the Saturday, about eight people arrived, and we had all the major items of furniture shifted into my new quarters in less than an hour.

Soon after I moved into this apartment, my daughter Elaine asked if I would take the piano which had been in storage for about five years. The piano is actually mine, but she had had the use of it while I was traveling and living overseas. It is an English Mason Rich upright grand piano, built in 1896, and still in good condition. She and Steve were finding it too expensive to pay the cost of the storage, and she knew I missed being able to play.

This move was quite an experience. I had hired a local firm to do the work, and I knew it wouldn't be an easy job, as there are fourteen stairs up to my apartment, straight in from the front door. As it turned out, the stairs weren't a problem. Bob Sommers and his crew laid cushioning all the way up the stairs, roped the piano once it was inside the door, and dragged it up fairly easily. It was maneuvering it around three sharp corners into the living room which proved the worst job. They finally upended the piano, brought it into the living room around all the corners, set it down and pushed it into place against one of the long walls. Whew!

Chapter 3

CHURCH AND COMMUNITY

As I mentioned earlier, I had started attending Christian Fellowship Center on Village Way in Qualicum soon after I came home from my last six months in Kona. The pastor, Brian Robertson, suggested that I ask Dorothy Lawrence, an older lady, if she would be willing to drive me to and from church. She agreed, and we are still traveling together each week.

I love being a part of CFC, as we call it. It is a very friendly congregation, and supports eight different missionary efforts in different parts of the world, as well as taking care of those in need within its own congregation.

I soon found I could be useful as both an usher and a greeter, and eventually became responsible for making out the schedules for both. I also became involved in leading a team of friends in Sunday afternoon services at the various seniors' homes in the Qualicum area. Within two years, I was also planning the schedules for those, but that only lasted for two years. It just became too complicated. Now, the minister at the local Baptist church makes out the schedules, and I just have to share them with my colleagues on the CFC team.

As part of my work for the church, I helped out when we had love-feasts or seders for various reasons, and especially when we opened our doors in early December to the whole community for a pre-Christmas dinner. They took a lot of preparation, from the assembling of enough turkeys and hams and vegetables and desserts—enough to feed approximately six hundred people or more—to the setting up and decoration of the auditorium and the tables.

CFC has several different worship teams which lead the services on Sundays. There is also a dance team which uses movement to portray the emotions of the songs we sing during those services. We have a lively Sunday School for children from three years old to teenagers, and a nursery where parents of very young children can go to nurse or play with their infants. There is also a library with about eight hundred books, available for free borrowing.

From time to time, we become involved in public events such as the local Family Day in late May, and the July 1st Canada Day parade in Parksville. We have many guest speakers, both on Sunday mornings and presenting workshops during the week from time to time.

Since I joined this congregation, I have become involved with three different home groups. Two of them broke up at different times because the leaders moved away from Vancouver Island, but the third one is still going strong.

We meet one evening each week at one member's house, and share worship songs, talk about and pray for each other's problems, and enjoy some Bible study and teaching.

Our leaders are very active in both the Christian Chiropractors' group and the Gideons' Bible Society, so they travel to other countries two or three times a year, and bring back stories of their encounters to share with the group.

*   *   *

During these past ten years, I have worked as a volunteer in a number of community offices. One of these was the Community Policing Office, which is located in the town hall. I was doing a regular weekly shift for about five years, making Keep In Touch (KIT) calls when I was on the morning shift, and answering questions and providing information to any visitors.

The KIT calls went out daily to a number of people who were living alone, perhaps recovering from surgery, or just needing someone to keep in touch. I also helped put together what we called Medical Alert Kits or MAK packs. These contained several leaflets with important information, especially for older people, and a vial containing a sheet of personal and medical information which the user would fill in. The vial would be put in their refrigerator, and a sticky label attached to the frig door. This would alert ambulance crews to which medications the person was taking and what, if any, medical conditions they were suffering on a long term basis.

Another group I worked with was the local Cancer Society. It was mostly a case of being available to provide information to those who had cancer, or had a relative with cancer. I found out, soon after I joined, that they had several boxes of photographs and news items from about the ten previous years. These needed arranging in date order and putting into albums, and I was happy to do this for them.

A third volunteer group I joined at another time was the local Hospice society. We don't have any hospice beds in the house where the members meet, but many of our members visited one on one with people who were ill, or who had Alzheimer's or other serious conditions. We also have several members who work in the Palliative Care unit at the Nanaimo hospital. I had one particular patient in a local Seniors' home who was approaching her 100th birthday. I visited her and prayed for her at least once a week for two and a half years. She finally died six weeks after her all-important birthday. Her daughter told me she thought that Astrid had just been waiting for that before she would let go.

One of my favorite activities was accompanying the choir from the local Seniors' Activity Center. I was asked to become their regular pianist in March 2007, and stayed with them until December 2010. The conductor during the first two years was Don Turner, a very lively 80-year-old, who really knew his music. He not only "stretched" the choir to achieve more than they thought they could; some of the accompaniments really stretched me!

About once or twice a month we would visit one of the local seniors' homes, and give a program. The pieces ranged from musical stage and film pieces to traditional British folk songs—and everything in between. One or two of our singers would give the choir a rest by singing a solo or duet, and occasionally, one of our gentlemen would perform a recitation such as "Albert and the Lion". Don himself was really good at that.

After I had been with the choir about two years, Don and his wife moved to Chemainus, but he had trained a good friend of his, Lynn Beamond to take over. Her methods were different from Don's, but the choir and I soon settled into a new routine. I had to leave the choir in December 2010, as arthritis was taking its toll on my hands. They presented me with several gifts and a bouquet of flowers. One of the gifts was a plaque which reads, "Music is a lifelong friend". It isn't very big, but they all managed to sign the back of it.

Chapter 4

MORE TRAVELS

In March of 2009, I had the pleasure of going to Israel for the first time. The YWAM Associates International group was holding a Renewal Conference there for the first time ever. I had been to two of these while I was in Australia, and was eager to go to this one. We stayed at the Yad Hashmona guest house complex, about fifteen minutes' drive from Jerusalem. This was quite a remarkable place, as there was a reconstructed Biblical village in the grounds. There were over fifty YWAMers from fifteen countries attending the conference. Our speaker was Dr. David Demian, from "Watchmen for the Nations", and he was a very interesting and knowledgeable person.

We had worship and intercession, followed by a teaching session in the mornings, and made several trips out in the afternoons. On the Monday afternoon, we went by coach to the Old City of Jerusalem, and looked out from the rebuilt fortress of the City of David. Our guide then took us down into Hezekiah's tunnel leading to the Gishon Spring, by which King David had been able to enter, attack and conquer the city so many years ago.

Then the guide showed us where the Pool of Siloam had been, followed by a visit to the Western Wall of Solomon's Temple, the only remaining part of that building after the 70 A.D. destruction by the Romans. The guide showed us the seven hundred pound solid gold menorah, which modern-day Jews had acquired, as one of the objects which would be placed in a new Temple which they hoped to build. Then he led us into the upper part of the city to the building where the Upper Room was said to have been.

On Tuesday afternoon, we started at the Mount of Olives, walked through the Garden of Gethsemane with its two-thousand-year old olive trees to the Church of St. Anne. This was supposed to have some of the best acoustics in the world. Of course, we had to try them out. It was marvelous! We also stopped by the Pool of Bethesda and took Communion, before going up the last part of the way to Calvary. We followed the route Jesus had taken with His cross, along the Via Dolorosa, walking over some of the original paving stones which had been specially preserved. We finished our tour at the site of Golgotha, and the Garden Tomb.

**View of Jerusalem from the
Mount of Olives**

On Wednesday afternoon, we traveled south of Jerusalem to the Dead Sea. We called in at the ancient site of Tel Megiddo, and walked over one of the same pathways which King Solomon had used. We visited the fortress of Masada, and then stopped at the oasis of Engedi. We had brought a packed lunch, which we ate by the sea, and some of us went into the water to test its buoyancy. On the way back, we also went to Qum Ran, the site where the "Dead Sea Scrolls" were found, back in 1949.

Some of our group went to the Holocaust Memorial on Thursday afternoon, but I chose not to go. I needed some time to contemplate all we had already seen and heard. It was truly a case of history coming to life, and somewhat overwhelming.

On Friday evening, we had a "Welcoming Shabbat" ceremony in the dining room, led by the leader of the education facility. He told us, in English and Hebrew, the history of the sacrament, and explained each step. Then he passed out loaves of bread and cups of wine for us to share. It was a very moving experience.

Since it is not easy to get a plane out of Ben Gurion (Tel Aviv) airport on a Saturday, the Jewish Sabbath, most of the group had agreed to wait an extra day. The YWAM group leaders had arranged for us to take a whole day tour north to the Galilee. We stopped at Mount Carmel, but were not allowed to walk in the grounds of the monastery. So we had a session of prayer and intercession just outside. Then we went on to Capernaum, saw where St. Peter had lived, and visited the restored remains of the synagogue. Next, we went to the shore of Lake Galilee and rode in a "Jesus boat", with some of the crew singing traditional Hebrew songs. Some of the ladies in our group joined in dancing a *hora* to the music. That was quite a day!

"Jesus boat" on the Sea of Galilee

Since we were staying in a guest house complex about forty-five minutes' drive from the airport, our leaders wanted to use as few taxi-coaches as possible to take us there. Unfortunately, this meant that I had to leave at 2 a.m. on Sunday morning, and travel with two couples, one of whom was headed to Norway, and the other to Denmark. Their plane left two hours before mine, and I had a five hour wait. I had several hours' layover at Heathrow, and by the time I arrived at the hotel in Vancouver, I had been on the go for over thirty hours. I just could not haul my suitcase up the five steps into the hotel lobby, but the clerk saw my problem and came to help. He rewarded me with a room which had a Jacuzzi in the bathroom. It was well worth the wait for the tub to fill, even though it was after midnight by then.

*   *   *

In May 2010, I took Rose to England with me, as she had never been. (I had been making trips there about every four years since 1963.) We landed at Gatwick airport in London at 6:30 on a Sunday morning, and needed to take a train to Reading, and then on to Plymouth. The powers that be changed the platform for our train at the last minute. I grabbed my suitcases, and left my copper cane leaning on the bench where we had been waiting. I didn't realize I had left it behind until we were getting off the train in Plymouth.

When we arrived at Joan's house, I told her what had happened. She suggested we go to Boots chemists shop in the city the next morning, and see if they could help. They had several canes, but not of the kind I needed to support my balance. (No joint problems, thank goodness!) One of the assistants suggested we try the market. As soon as we entered, we saw a stall with a barrel full of beautifully decorated canes. I chose one, and still have it. I've had lots of compliments about it, as well as questions as to where I had bought it.

While we were in Plymouth, I took Rose down to the Barbican, which is what remains of the old part of the city. I showed her where the *Mayflower* had sailed from several hundred years ago, and we visited an Elizabethan garden, which has been kept up until today. We also walked on Plymouth Hoe, and then wandered through the city from a different angle from the first day. Another day, we took the train to Penzance and ate lunch in a café there. Then we took a bus out to Marazion, and walked across the sands to St. Michael's Mount.

After five days with my sister and her husband, we traveled to Harpenden in Hertfordshire, to stay at the British National YWAM base for a few days. While we were there, Rose and I spent one day in London, walking from Westminster Bridge to Trafalgar Square, and then taking a boat ride on the Thames. We also went to the Tower of London and toured the Crown Jewels display.

My friend Joy, who had been my room-mate in Crossroads, now lived in Harpenden, and we spent most of the Sunday with her. She had promised to take us out for lunch, which we ate at a local pub.

Our trip finished with a visit to Chesterfield, where we stayed in a B & B which I had used before. I was able to show Rose the house where I grew up, the school I went to, and the chapel I had attended. We walked through the Queen's Park, where Dad and I had been to many cricket matches, and spent some time in town, with a visit to the Norman Parish Church with its "Crooked Spire" towering several hundred feet above the nearby buildings. The weathervane cockerel on the top is several feet out of plumb, and was only rescued in the late 1950's when a local surveying firm found that, of the four ancient oak beams on which it was mounted, only half of one beam was left. The repairs were costly, but the spire still stands proud.

*   *   *

In early June 2011, Rose and I took a trip to Prince Edward Island and Nova Scotia. I flew from Comox to Calgary, and stayed overnight with Rose and Bob. It was quite a surprise, when we checked in for our flight to Halifax, to see Guy arriving to work in Calgary for a few days.

We landed in Halifax about 6:30 a.m., picked up our luggage, and ate breakfast while at the airport. Rose had reserved a car, and we were soon on our way north. We had a short nap partway to the Confederation Bridge (over twelve kilometers in length!), and arrived at our hotel in Charlottetown by noon.

After eating breakfast at the hotel, we headed for the Visitors' Centre downtown. There were no bus tours of the city available, so we spent most of the morning walking around the central area.

On Tuesday, we drove to Cavendish. Rose had always been a fan of the "Anne of Green Gables" books, and dearly wanted to see where Lucy Maud Montgomery lived. We toured the house where the author had grown up, and then went to the beach. After enjoying a lobster-roll lunch, we returned to the hotel by a different route.

**Rose outside the home of Lucy Maud
Montgomery, Cavendish**

On Wednesday, we were able to tour Confederation
Hall, and then set out along Hwy. #1 to Woods Island for
the ferry to Pictou, Nova Scotia. It was pouring rain by the
time we landed, so we made a stop for supper at Baddeck,
hoping the rain would not be so bad when we had finished.
It was only about thirty kilometers from there to Sydney,
and our next hotel.

The next day, we drove to the old French fortress of
Louisbourg. A shuttle bus took us from the reception center
to the fortress itself, which is actually a fortified town. In
each of the main buildings, there were people dressed in 18th
century costumes from the period when the French were
fighting the English over their last Canadian possession.
We spent a couple of hours wandering through various
buildings and talking to the costumed volunteers. Then we
took the shuttle bus back to the reception area, and walked
through the gallery of paintings and photographs depicting
the main points of the history of the fortress.

On the Friday, we left the hotel early so that we could drive the Cabot Trail. The countryside was gorgeous, and the weather warm but not too hot. After driving up the east side, we stopped at Wreck Beach for a seafood lunch. Then we followed the highway to Neil's Harbor, across and south to Cheticamp. I had a slight accident when we stopped to take an unusual photo on one of the bays. I fell down a gravel bank and scraped one knee and one elbow. So we stopped in Baddeck on the way back to Sydney, and I was able to get first aid from one of the drug store assistants there.

The next day, we drove into downtown Sydney and walked along historic Charlotte Street. Then we went down to the harbor for a while. In the afternoon, we drove to St. Peter's, where we stopped at the old canal lock. On the way back, we stopped for oatcakes and tea at Rita MacNeil's tearoom.

The day after that, it was time to head back to Halifax. We stopped for lunch in Antigonish, and then went on through New Glasgow and Truro to Bedford. Our new hotel was located between there and Halifax, on the airport side of the city.

On our first day in Halifax, we started in the harbor area at the Visitors' Center. We decided to take the "Harbor Hopper" tour, which gave us a view of the main places of interest in the city, and also included an amphibious trip on the harbor itself for about ten minutes. Once back on land, we spent more time in the same area, exploring the "Historical Properties" beside the water, and eating lunch there.

The next day, we traveled to Peggy's Cove, and walked over to the lighthouse. From there, we went to Lunenberg, where we ate lunch at the "Scuttlebutt" Café. The *Bluenose II* was under canvas for major repairs and upgrading, so we didn't get to see her. However, there was another ship of the same era in dock, and we had a look at her. We were back at our hotel by about 4 p.m.

On the following day, we visited the Crystal Gallery, where there were some really beautiful gems and jewelry. Then we went to the citadel for a tour, and were in time to watch the firing of the Noon Gun. We walked through the beautiful Public Gardens, and cruised around the buildings of Dalhousie University, where my grand-daughter Nicole has been studying for the past three years. That evening, we ate supper in Bedford at the "True North Diner", and spent a quiet evening in the hotel.

We had two more days left, and made the most of them. First of all, we went to Pier 21, where thousands of immigrants had landed and been processed in past years. There was an excellent video showing some of the incidents of those days, and an interesting gallery of displays and individual items which the people might have brought with them.

In the afternoon, we went to the Natural History Museum, which was quite impressive.

On our last "free" morning, we drove across the Alexander Mackay Bridge to Dartmouth, and took a tour of a recreated Quaker house from the last century. We traveled back to the hotel around the head of Bedford Basin. We ate supper in Halifax, and drove back to the hotel via a different route from those we had used before. Altogether, we had seen much of the Halifax, Dartmouth and Bedford area.

It took only about half an hour, the next morning, to drive to the airport and return our rented car, and there were no problems. The flight to Calgary was a smooth one, and we landed on time. I spent a quiet day the next day, mostly reorganizing the things I had taken with us, and packing ready to return home.

Chapter 5

RETURN TO KONA

Early in 2011, I started making arrangements to go back to Kona for "six months less a day". This is all I am allowed to do without having to obtain a "green card" (U.S. working permit). After several weeks of back and forth correspondence with the Staff Services office, I received confirmation of my wish to be there from early October until late March 2012. I knew I would be working under Madge Bridges, who had been my boss in the library in the six months I worked there in 2000-2001.

My travel agent had told me that her company only worked with one travel medical insurance company. When we checked into their rates, they wanted $5,600 for 179 days, with a $500 deductible. I told Michelle I would do some further research. I finally came up with a company which charged me $2,600 with only a $250 deductible.

On October 3, I met my friend Deborah at a local café for breakfast, and then we started driving to the ferry at Duke Point, south of Nanaimo. The ferry brought us to Tsawassan on the Vancouver side, and we were able to go from there to the Peace Arch border crossing. We stopped for a picnic lunch, and then crossed into the U.S. without problems.

I had booked us into a hotel near the Seattle airport, and we checked in about 5 p.m. We ate dinner at a nearby Denny's restaurant, but I was just too tired to finish my meal. We were up by 6:30, ate breakfast at the hotel, and headed for the airport. Deborah helped me check in, and we had coffee together before she left to return to Vancouver and then to the Island.

The flight to Kona was smooth and easy. Madge met me there, and took me to my new "home" in one of the dormitory suites at the top of the campus. I was sharing a bedroom with a Japanese American lady, and there were two other staff ladies in the second bedroom. We had a living room/kitchen area and a bathroom which the four of us shared.

From then on, I walked down to the open patio for breakfast each morning about 6:15, and started work in the library at 8:30. I had a few problems at first, as the computer cataloguing system was completely different from the one I had used eleven years before.

On one of my first mornings, Madge had said, "It will take you two months to master this, and then I'll have four months of good work out of you."

It worked out just about like that. In the six months I was there, I was able to catalogue the books which were waiting when I arrived, a whole bunch of new books which we ordered in January, and also go through ten boxes of books which had been in storage for several years without being catalogued. I don't think Madge was unhappy.

We also had quite a bit of fun. A couple of Fridays, Madge declared as "Aloha Fridays", and we dressed up in Hawaiian skirts, leis, and artificial flowers, and went across to the café for cold drinks, which Madge paid for. The kindergarten children visited us twice while I was there. One time was just before the Christmas break, when they came to sing carols.

There was also a lot of construction going on. Teams of Mennonites from Pennsylvania came to put up another dormitory building, and also to help build a new combined cafeteria/bakery with a visual arts centre in the lowest level. This could have been threatened when a car missed the road junction just outside the campus, overturned and started a fire. It spread through thirty-seven acres of the dry grass and scrub just outside our fence, but the grounds crew had cut fire-breaks in the immediate area, and the campus property wasn't touched at all.

As usual, while I was in Kona, I took a couple of breaks over a long weekend each time. I made one trip by bus to Hilo, on the north side of the Island, and stayed in a B&B which had a Japanese theme. My room had bamboo cane chairs, and Japanese prints on the wall. There was a tiny stream running through the garden behind the house, and koi fish swimming in it.

Hilo is quite an historic town, and I had a good time wandering around and renewing my acquaintance with it. I walked up to the Rainbow Falls, and took a couple of photos. The next day I went out to one of the big shopping malls. I had been told to wait for the bus back to Kona in a certain place, only to see it go by on the other side of the road. There was only the one bus, each day, so I had to stay an extra night.

During Christmas week, I flew to the Island of Kauai. This was the one major island in the Hawaiian chain which I had never visited. It was SO different from all the others. There was the capital city of Lihue, where the airport was located, and then there were sheer mountains dividing the north from the south side of the island. I spent most of one day in Lihue, but I decided that, in order to see the rest of the area, I had to take a helicopter tour. So I did!

One weekend, I stayed in Kona, in the same hotel where we had been housed when we came back from the Crossroads Outreach in 1995. On the Saturday, I joined a "Round the Island" bus tour. We visited an orchid factory, a macadamia nut outlet, and a lovely bakery which had been in existence for over fifty years, among other places. We also made a stop in Volcanoes National Park, walked through a lava tube, and were able to view the steaming caldera from a safe distance. We finished up with a walk on Black Sand Beach, and a quick visit to an old-established coffee mill and café. As you probably know, Kona coffee is world famous.

The next day, I went to the Congregational Church near the waterfront, where my friend Ruth joined me. Then I took a whale-watching tour in the afternoon. We were fortunate, as we saw two different pods of humpback whales, and they were very active. That was quite a weekend!

All too soon, my time in Kona came to an end, and Madge was tapping on my door, ready to take me to the airport. This time, I flew to Honolulu, and then took a direct overnight flight to Vancouver. My daughter Elaine was there to meet me, and take me to my grand-daughter's house for a good rest. I stayed with her overnight, and then Lynne drove me to the bus station. The bus from downtown took me to the ferry, and Ernest was waiting for me when I arrived in Nanaimo.

Chapter 6

LAST WORDS

I have now been home in Qualicum Beach for about five months, and I am gradually settling back into my usual routine. I have taken up several of my jobs with Christian Fellowship Church again, and I do an occasional volunteer shift at the Community Policing office.

My arthritis won't allow me to play the piano very much, but I still do play occasionally. I have also had to "ration" my time on the computer for the same reason.

I am hoping to go back to Kona next February, just for a week with some of my old friends. Then I am also hoping to make another tour to Israel in May 2013. This one will be organized by our missionary friends, Jay and Meridel Rawlings.

I know my life is safe in the good Lord's hands, and I am content to have it that way.

**75th Birthday cake at family party,
June 2010**

**Family gathering in 2012
(Lynne and her family not here)**

Appendix

YWAM Is . . .

The letters Y-W-A-M stand for "Youth With A Mission"—and that means 'youth' of all ages. There are people active in the organization from what we call 'King's Kids' to people in their 70's and early 80's.

YWAM is an international interdenominational organization, which was started by a man named Loren Cunningham. Back in the early 40's, he had a vision of waves of young people being swept up onto the beaches of the Third World, particularly in south-east and south Asia. He was eventually able to bring a group of people together, buy some land on the Big Island of Hawaii, near the town of Kona, and start building a campus.*

The primary aim was to train young people to go out as missionaries to the nations of the world where the Gospel is little known, but it has since become much more than that.

The organization has grown until it now has offices or bases in over 200 countries around the world.

The original name that Loren and his committee gave to the Kona campus was "Pacific and Asia Christian University" (PACU), but this was later changed to "University of the Nations" (UofN).

By the time I went to Kona in 1994 that was our International base. Wherever there is a campus, rather than just an office, courses are offered from a Christian perspective on subjects relating to the seven 'mind molders' of Education, Business, Arts, Religion, Family, Government and Communications. The basic Discipleship Training School (DTS) is a prerequisite for almost every other course.

The people found on campus will be in one of three categories: Mission Builders, staff, or students.

*   *   *

For more details about Loren and the beginnings of YWAM, see his first book, *Is that Really You, God?*

Mission Builders are those who visit a YWAM campus for anywhere from three weeks to three months at a time as volunteer workers. In many cases, they only need their airfare and personal expenses. Housing and meals are provided. Many of these people are retired, but not all. Some are young people looking for something worthwhile to do in a Christian environment.

They may work as plumbers, carpenters, electricians, telephone mechanics or operators, auto mechanics, building maintenance people, librarians, accountants, secretaries, child-care workers, cooks, cleaners, hospitality people, gardeners or grounds keepers. Each department has one or more staff persons responsible for assigning and supervising the work.

Some Mission Builders return year after year, to the Kona campus or elsewhere. Working as a Mission Builder is a great way to "test the waters" of YWAM, and decide if you want to go further within the organization.

Staff members are in two categories. There are those who teach courses in the various colleges, just like a secular university. There are also "operational staff" who supervise the areas where the Mission Builders work. In order to go on staff, a person must have completed a DTS, including the Outreach phase following the classroom course.

Students are those doing a DTS, or a second or third level course in the subject areas of humanities, communications, family ministries, counseling, Bible study, primary health care, audio or video technology, the arts or photography.

Most classroom courses run for three months, followed by a three-month Outreach period. So there is a "Transition week" four times a year in Kona. One exception is the nine months' long School of Bible Studies, which has no Outreach. Another is TESOL (Teaching English to Students of Other Languages). This school runs for six weeks, and there is no prerequisite training to do. TESOL students often go out to use their secular professional work as a means of passing on the Gospel message to those whom they meet day by day. Many of them choose to work in Third World countries.

One remarkable thing about YWAM is that nobody receives a salary. Everyone, from the Chancellor on down is a volunteer, either self-supporting or mission supported.

Any YWAM campus is a wonderful place to be, if only because there can be people from many different countries living and working together at any one time. In the January 2012 term while I was last in Kona, there were over five hundred students from 44 countries on base. It is a great place to learn about other cultures, and to share your own.

Once I left Kona in March 2001, I became a member of the Associates International. There is an email newsletter published every month, and seminars are held in various parts of the world several times each year.

* * *